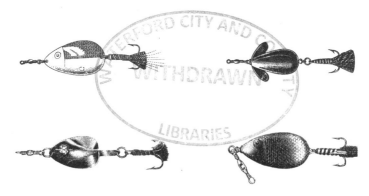

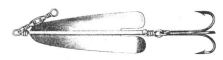

OUT
OF THE
BLUE

OUT
OF THE
BLUE

On Fishing at Sea

CHRIS
YATES

HAMISH HAMILTON
an imprint of
PENGUIN BOOKS

HAMISH HAMILTON

Published by the Penguin Group
Penguin Books Ltd, 80 Strand, London WC2R 0RL, England
Penguin Group (USA) Inc., 375 Hudson Street, New York, New York 10014, USA
Penguin Group (Australia), 250 Camberwell Road, Camberwell, Victoria 3124, Australia
(a division of Pearson Australia Group Pty Ltd)
Penguin Group (Canada), 90 Eglinton Avenue East, Suite 700, Toronto, Ontario, Canada M4P 2Y3
(a division of Pearson Penguin Canada Inc.)
Penguin Ireland, 25 St Stephen's Green, Dublin 2, Ireland (a division of Penguin Books Ltd)
Penguin Books India Pvt Ltd, 11 Community Centre, Panchsheel Park, New Delhi – 110 017, India
Penguin Group (NZ), 67 Apollo Drive, Rosedale, North Shore 0632, New Zealand
(a division of Pearson New Zealand Ltd)
Penguin Books (South Africa) (Pty) Ltd, 24 Sturdee Avenue, Rosebank, Johannesburg 2196, South Africa

Penguin Books Ltd, Registered Offices: 80 Strand, London WC2R 0RL, England

www.penguin.com

First published 2008
2

Illustrations copyright © William Yates, Clare Hatcher, Clare Shepherd
William Yates: 2nd, 6th, 9th, 12th, 14th, 15th, 16th, 17th, 18th and 19th casts.
Clare Hatcher: 4th cast.
Clare Shepherd: 5th and 22nd cast.

Text copyright © Chris Yates, 2008

The moral right of the author has been asserted

Set in Monotype Dante
Typeset by Rowland Phototypesetting Ltd, Bury St Edmunds, Suffolk
Printed in Great Britain by Clays Ltd, St Ives plc

A CIP catalogue record for this book is available from the British Library

ISBN: 978-0-241-14362-9

www.greenpenguin.co.uk

To Matt, who gave me a key to the sea.

Do they ever meet out there,
The dolphins I counted,
The otter I wait for?
I should have spent my life
Listening to the waves.

Michael Longley, *Out There*

CONTENTS

FIRST CAST   *The Gravity of the Sea*   1

SECOND CAST   *Since the Tide Turned*   7

THIRD CAST   *Ripples and Shadows*   13

FOURTH CAST   *The Fish That Smiled*   19

FIFTH CAST   *This Evening*   35

SIXTH CAST   *Home from the Sea*   47

SEVENTH CAST   *A Rock Too Far*   57

EIGHTH CAST   *Out of the Blue*   67

NINTH CAST   *The Tidal River*   73

TENTH CAST   *The Sea Perch*   81

ELEVENTH CAST   *Shark Bait*   91

TWELFTH CAST   *Something Out There*   101

CONTENTS

THIRTEENTH CAST	*Atlantis*	111
FOURTEENTH CAST	*The History of a Plug*	123
FIFTEENTH CAST	*Mackerel and Old Oak*	131
SIXTEENTH CAST	*The Void Sea*	139
SEVENTEENTH CAST	*Sublime Choices*	147
EIGHTEENTH CAST	*The Hour Before Sunrise*	157
NINETEENTH CAST	*Sunrise and Sea Monsters*	165
TWENTIETH CAST	*Seascape With Broken Rod*	173
TWENTY-FIRST CAST	*Sea Changes*	183
TWENTY-SECOND CAST	*Hoping for the Best*	191

Acknowledgements

To Simon Benham, who read some notes I'd sketched out down by the sea and encouraged me to develop them into a book; to Simon Prosser, who agreed to publish it; to Juliette Mitchell, who read each chapter as I finished it and whose editorial insight straightened a few wobbly casts; to my son Will for producing some crisp illustrations; and finally to my friends, both wet and dry, who helped with the voyage to the final page.

FIRST
CAST

*The
Gravity
of the
Sea*

Fishing in an old overgrown pond yesterday, hoping for a fat green tench, I couldn't help thinking of the sea. There were no waves on the surface, no ripples even, and I was thirty miles from the coast; the stillness, however, revealed a just perceptible current, and every ten or so minutes I had to adjust my float, a painted goose quill, which kept swinging gently round with the flow, trying to join the small queue of floating leaves and bits of twig heading for the exit, a narrow spillway in the centre of the dam. Quietly, the water gurgled over the outfall, feeding a stream that meandered out of sight, flowing east then south towards the English Channel.

Because the sway of my float got me thinking how a still pool could never be still, I began to feel the pull of the sea, like gravity, drawing everything, including me, towards it. Had the quill vanished below the surface, no doubt this idea would have gone down with it, but during the hours while I waited for a bite my thoughts ran like a migratory eel down the spillway. Eventually, a slight movement of leaves over my head created a sound like distant waves and I convinced myself there was a salt smell in the air.

Such is the quality of that pond – my favourite tench water, with all the traditional elements of willows, reeds and lilies perfectly in place – it seemed an act of betrayal to be thinking about somewhere else, especially somewhere like a different planet, but these last few years I've obviously been suffering from a kind of seasonal disorder. And now it's struck again.

It is July, yet just when I've begun the annual happy round of summer watering holes the sea rises in my imagination and tries to flood them all. It's not that I could ever become bored or overfamiliar with the half-dozen lakes and ponds that have been providing my dreams with their staple diet these last fifty years. And it is only usually at times like yesterday, when one of those waters is dreaming itself, when nothing will wake it, that I get this needling seagull call in my head.

In the past, if I felt I needed a change of scene during the summer, I would always switch from still to running water, though I preferred – and still prefer – to save the rivers for the autumn when the big perch begin to move. Nowadays, however, if the tench and carp – my favourite summer species – are not responding, I only think of the rivers when I drive alongside them, down their valleys towards the sea.

Like many other freshwater anglers, I organized my fishing in accordance with a piscine calendar: perch and grayling in winter; trout in spring; carp (especially crucian carp) and tench in summer; barbel and perch (again) in autumn. This made for ever-changing yet beautifully predictable seasons full of contrasting colours and character and differently charged atmospheres. My only complaint was that, living in an angler's paradise, it was often difficult juggling parenthood and work on the one hand and devout fish worship on the other. And now, even as I savour the green incense of a tench pond, I'm distracted by this new infatuation with the big untameable serene unpredictable deep blue sea.

SECOND
CAST

*Since
the Tide
Turned*

Yesterday I wasn't catching anything from a small pond, today I'm not catching anything from the sea, but there the continuity ends. Yesterday was green, dappled and intimate; today is blue, glittering and expansive. If contrast in itself is a stimulant then I should be fizzing by now, and probably would be if there was a fish to make the difference complete.

When I set out this morning, there was a slight northerly breeze which is now unnoticeable at the foot of these south-facing cliffs. The sky is cloudless, but though it is a fine day to be by the sea, conditions are not ideal for the sort of fishes I like to cast for.

They respond to the sea's energy, but if there is no energy an entire shoal can just drift and dissolve like smoke. They need stirring up, they need rough water, but the surface is unruffled, and instead of breaking waves the sea's edge is defined by a series of long slow incoming ripples which glint and create a few bubbles and make a sound like wading cattle. Because of the calm the water is beautifully clear. I'm sitting on a sun-warmed boulder, and if I look down I can see to the bottom of a deep channel where the seaweed hardly sways and only prawns or crabs flit or crawl over the stony bed.

My rod and net lie on the rock next to me. I'm having a break from the fishing, jotting down these notes while, at the same time, crunching an apple, which is all I brought with me for lunch. It's early afternoon and, probably because it's a long and slightly treacherous walk down from the cliffs and round to this small cove, I have the place to myself. Half a mile offshore a sailing boat is doing its best to gather what breeze there is, but it seems to be moving slower than the piece of driftwood that floats towards me on the tide.

Occasional gulls glide overhead and, just then, the rock walls behind me echoed with the calls of three oystercatchers that have now landed amongst nearby rock pools. All the while I'm hoping to see or hear something that will make me pick up the rod again. If the fish come in, as they usually do with the tide, they may break surface as they pursue shoals of sand eels or other small prey, and on a quiet day like today, even if I'm not looking, like now, I'll hear the commotion and so mark the spot for a hurried cast. This last hour, since the tide turned, I've been roaming along the water's edge, casting, but with no response; then I scanned the bay with binoculars and watched to see if the gulls were circling in a particular area, but there's been nothing to feed my optimism. However I'm still optimistic enough, and I've certainly not begun to wonder whether I should head back inland to the tench pond. Despite the sea's indifference to me, I'm happy just being in its presence and would not really care if the conditions remained unchanged until sunset, though of course, because of the tides, everything is always changing.

Whether or not I get a chance of a fish, there's still a

lot to see and, now I'm looking, a lot to remember, because these limpets scattered over this rock, this sepia-coloured seaweed, these overflowing tide pools are all reminding me that I've been here before, that this new adventure actually began quite a long time ago.

THIRD
CAST

*Ripples and
Shadows*

Just like millions of others on this island country, I was splashing about along a summer beach almost before I could walk. My first impression of the sea was of a fantastic horizontal shimmering of light, and, like most small children who have not actually grown up by the coast, I was as much terrified as delighted. For all the subsequent years of my childhood, the sea never disappointed, but I only ever saw it in summer, when it was mostly benign. The sea was August, with long beaches, sandcastles and ice cream, although my clearest memories of it concern more remote, rugged shorelines, away from crowds and coastal towns, where the receding tide would sometimes reveal extraordinary landscapes.

Around the age of four or five, the period of my life when the world first began to speak to me about real things, like owls, lizards and sticklebacks, my family went for a fortnight's holiday along a favourite stretch of coast near Exmouth; and one rather gloomy drizzly day we went by ferry and steam train to Teignmouth, where my father said there were smugglers' tunnels and caves. It was true, there was a tunnel and several sea caves, but there was also an extensive area of rocks, ledges and tide pools which I started to explore even while my sister, Helen, and brother, Nick, were still making their voices echo in the caves behind me.

After hopping over the rocks for a bit, poking about for shells and small crabs, I came to a gulley that was too wide to jump – or, rather, too deep to jump. It ran between weed-festooned ridges for about twenty yards and then shallowed before it reached the open sea. Carefully I picked my way along the slippery edges, looking down into the dark clear water. The channel narrowed and, because the tide was out, it was blocked by layers of piled kelp which I used as a causeway to get to the opposite side. The rock pool was the deepest I had ever seen, too deep to see everything on the bottom. I could make out a few large grey stones, and there was a patch of pale sand across which something swayed like a flag-sized band of seaweed caught by a current. As it moved again I focused more sharply. For a second, I actually wanted to believe it *was* seaweed because surely nothing so incredible – a fish as big as me – could live in a rock pool. It seemed to suddenly quiver its tail, then it dematerialized, and though I remained crouched on the edge of the pool, shouting for the others, I didn't see it again.

I'd seen fish in tide pools before, but they were all finger-length blennies and butterfish; the creature in the gulley was, by comparison, colossal. Whatever it was it confirmed that the mysterious potential of water was as genuine as I had always imagined. Afterwards, it was sometimes enough simply to narrow my gaze towards a place where I sensed a monster might lie and, as if forming out of ripples and shadows, the image of a great fish would appear before my eyes. No doubt, some of these were fantasies, but most of them were real, like the fish which was almost certainly a big salmon that swam out from under a landing stage on the Exe estuary, and the trio of wonderful spectral-looking creatures – probably bass – that drifted close by me as I was watching from a rock near Salcombe. The idea of casting a line and trying to connect with any of these marvels was just too hair-raising a prospect to even consider, not that I had a line or a rod to cast it with. But then, perhaps the greatest surprise of all, I discovered monsters in the village pond, back at home, a miracle that finally led to the acquisition of my first fishing rod and the beginning of an obsession with carp. Yet though my first casts were into freshwater, my fishing tackle came with me as soon as we all went again to the sea.

FOURTH
CAST

*The
Fish That
Smiled*

The great advantage of fishing a stretch of coast which requires a bit of cliff hanging and rock scrambling to reach is that I often have the place to myself. And today, with this limitless expanse of sea before me and the uninhabited shoreline behind, it's easier to imagine that I've been marooned, and may even be the last person left on earth, than it is to realize there's a seaside town less than ten miles away with a beach seething with joyous humanity. Yet, as this place was once described to me by an-angler-who-knows as 'sometimes like a boiling fish kettle', I presumed I'd have the company of one or

two other fishermen by now; but then again maybe any angler worth his salt would not venture out here in these conditions.

Though I have, over the past few years, become more familiar with the marine environment, my salt content is not yet high enough for me to always interpret what the sea is saying. However, despite the fact that an ocean obviously has a much wider vocabulary than a pond or stream, my philosophy is the same wherever I fish. With the image of my chosen species clear in my head, I arrive at the water's edge impatient, enthusiatic, ready for anything (including nothing). And despite the fact that I have to view the sea with a wider focus than when I'm trying to read a river or lake, I can sometimes recognize the same promising signs in both. Occasionally, it's simply the quality of the light, or a particular texture on the surface, or a sense of something in the air – subtle, feeble indicators that can lead to a wonderful, even ludicrous confidence. On the other hand, there have been times when I don't seem able to grasp anything meaningful at all. This morning, when I arrived on the clifftop, the horizon-wide body of blue water looked magnificent, but all I saw in its expression was a kind of friendly blandness that didn't fill me with hope. In such settled conditions, however, the slightest fluctuation in current or breeze or light can sometimes change the direction of an entire shoal and bring them within casting range. And the prospect of high tide just before sunset made the blandness seem like a hidden promise. So, with the image of my favourite sea fish sinking only a little deeper in my expectations, I set off along the cliff path.

Hours have passed. When I arrived here the sea was retreating, leaving a glittering universe of different-shaped rock pools, but now the water is advancing and the pools have lost their identity to the government of tidal reform. My own rock will soon be overcome and I must withdraw to a neutral zone. Yet, despite the surge, the waves have become even more pathetic than before, giving the rising sea the appearance of a lake whose long-dormant springs had suddenly burst.

I'd prefer the sun to be a little lower in the sky yet, with high tide just over an hour away, I know I should be feeling more confident and more determined in my casting. Although the lack of visible indicators – no scatterings of small fish, no swirls on the calm surface, no dark shapes nosing between the newly drowned boulders – does not necessarily mean there are no fish in the area, I cast better when I have something to aim at. Perhaps I've been conditioned by my habit of never quite settling down until I either see or sense a definite opportunity. Presented with this same blank expanse of ripples on one of my freshwater haunts I would at least know what to do about it, even if it was only to pack up and go home. Despite being technically unsophisticated, my fifty years' experience on rivers and lakes obviously counts for something, but it can also make me blasé at times, as if there's no challenge I can't meet. And that is what excites me about the new seaward direction. Though some of my old skills will come in handy, I am in most senses a rank beginner, a true amateur, which is a happy state to be in. And if I flounder or hesitate at times, I can reassure myself by remembering what happened when, with hardly any angling experience of any kind, I first cast into the briny.

In the summer of my new fishing rod, when I was eleven, after I learnt how to catch tiddlers from my village pond, I went with my family on the annual sojourn to the south-west coast and, being ignorant of the ways of sea anglers, sought to educate myself by walking along the pier (the now rebuilt harbour jetty) at Weymouth to observe how the old salts caught their fish. My brother, Nick, who was nine and had also become wild about fish, came with me. We were amazed and rather depressed by what we saw: anglers with rods like scaffold poles, reels the size of lorry tyres, lines thick enough to moor a ship and lead weights heavy enough to anchor it. Next to such whale-stopping tackle, our rods seemed fit only for tickling shrimps. We spent almost a whole afternoon hoping to see a fisherman hook something worthy of his hauling gear, but if anyone caught a creature that wasn't a crab, it was always absurdly small. Intrigued, we returned a few days later, when the weather was wet and stormy, and it was wonderful to watch a heroic sou'westered figure, who had evidently been waiting for hours in the rain, finally reel in a brown flatfish no bigger than the palm of my hand. Pier fishing was, indeed, an eccentric, unproductive and extremely dull occupation, and even if we'd possessed the necessary heavy plant we decided not to attempt it.

We were staying for a fortnight on a farm only a few minutes' walk from Lulworth, so, putting aside ideas of casting from a pier, Nick and I began to explore the famous cove and the more rugged coastline to the west where, at low tide, there were rock pools with starfish. The cove was so sheltered from wind and wave it was like a millpond and our parents were quite happy to leave us there while we made our first saltwater casts. Someone on the farm had told us that sea fish could be taken on uncooked bacon, but though we stole two rashers from the kitchen we didn't even tempt a crab. It was exciting, nevertheless, especially when we cast from the cove's east side, where the fossilized forest slanted into deep water and where all kinds of Jurassic creatures were probably lurking. However, when you're young and crackling with expectancy, you quickly begin to distrust a place that doesn't live up to your fantasies. After a couple of hours we were convinced that no fish ever entered the cove – or at least none that recognized bacon.

The next day, leaving the rods at the farm, we

explored again the western coastline, where the energy of the open sea restored our hopes. It was low water when we reached our favourite bay and the tide pools were full of prawns, crabs and little fish. We splashed about, trying to catch blennies with our hands, and eventually waded into the edge of a wide shallow pool where something made us hesitate. What had appeared to be a ridge in the pool's centre moved. We stared, stepped forward and then jumped back as a sinuous green fish zigzagged into the air. Before we could do more than shout, the creature had skittered out of the water, floundered across a few layers of seaweed and thrashed itself into the sea. Yelling and howling, we danced after it, but it vanished into the foam.

Though it seemed like a monster at the time, it was probably just an overgrown mackerel or garfish, its startling jack-in-the-box appearance making it seem twice actual size. We weren't concerned with identification at the time; all that mattered was that the sea had revealed another marvel and told us exactly where to cast when the tide came in.

We bubbled with a new mad confidence, but we

would have to get hold of some proper bait and also persuade our parents to let us fetch our tackle and come back to the bay on our own. We'd heard about ragworms and lugworms, had seen the pier anglers using them, but had no idea where we might find them. We'd also watched a fisherman using a crab as bait, but that didn't seem quite feasible to us. There were plenty of limpets and other shellfish in the pools that every fish would surely appreciate as a crushable snack. We knocked a limpet off a rock with a stone, smashed it mercilessly and fed a few fragments to the elusive blennies, hiding under their ledges. They appeared so instantly, snapping up everything, fighting over the juicier bits, that knew we must have stumbled on the best bait in the world – or at least one that was better than bacon.

As we headed back to the farm for tea, the tide was turning, but with the extra push of a stiff onshore breeze the waves were building and crashing noisily, drowning all hopes of parental consent to our little plan. However, after tea I casually said that Nick and I might go down to the cove again for a few casts before sunset. Happy with the prospect of an hour's undisturbed reading, Mother wished us good luck and waved as we dawdled off through the farmhouse garden. But as soon as we were out of her sight, we ran down to the coastal path, then up the long slope to the edge of the cliffs and finally down again to the fish-haunted rocks.

Though we'd learnt through chill experience that you must always keep a watchful eye on the sea, we had no real idea of the height or frequency of the tides. So it was just good fortune that our return co-incided almost precisely with high water, when we could judge the safest casting position and when the fish would be coming in to feed virtually under our feet.

The sun would soon be behind the cliffs to our right and the sea was already a deep purplish blue. On the shoreward side of a row of jagged half-drowned boulders, fifty yards in front of us, the dark water was fanned across with white foam and spray as the waves hit them, reformed and surged on to-wards us. Standing on a great bungalow-sized rock, one that seemed well above the tideline, we set up our rods, sea style. It had been fine to use conventional freshwater rods in the placid cove, but they would never have coped with a riotous sea and a treacherous reef. So we converted them from three to two pieces, removing the slender top joint and creating solid eight-foot whopper-stoppers. Realizing that with lines of only nine-pound breaking strain we might lose a few hooks and weights, we'd collected a pocketful of stones with holes as alternatives to leads and just hoped we had enough hooks to last the evening. We dropped our limpet-baited tackle close in, where all but the larger waves were deflected by an out-facing ledge. Almost immediately we thought we were amongst fish. Our rods were pulled and dragged forward, but we soon discovered it was only the action of turbulence and undertow on our lines. We lost several hooks after they became snagged on rocks or in beds of wrack and kelp. After a while the large waves seemed to grow larger and fiercer, thumping into the underside of our rock and making it vibrate. The contrast between our previous angling experiences and this was like the difference between a bike ride through the woods at home and a bike ride round the rim of a volcano – with no brakes. *Whump!* went the wave, and the spray filled the air. Then the wave rebounded and swept away from us, colliding with the next incomer, forcing both skywards, creating more spray, which turned gold in the late sunlight. Our lines connected us physically with this spectacle, making it seem yet more intense, more powerful; and then, right in the centre of it, a different kind of tension – not the push or drag of the turbulence, but an edgy, increasing vibration that culminated in a terrific clout. The rod almost leapt out of my hands, but I held on tight and as the thumb-thick cane went into a sort of half-circle it was obvious I'd somehow hooked a fish – a *big* fish.

All the drama of the coast was concentrated down the line, and I was transfixed until both Nick and I started shouting simultaneously. In the few seconds I hadn't done anything, the fish had dived under a rock, but I managed to haul it free and it suddenly appeared on the surface. We started yelling again when we saw it swerving and splashing in the surf, for though this was not truly a monster it was easily the biggest thing I'd ever hooked.

We'd observed that real sea anglers never seemed

to carry landing nets; we didn't have one either, but when the fish came in under our boulder I didn't think I could lift it through the air. The problem was solved by a rising wave that, together with an extra lift of the rod, almost threw the creature onto my feet. I slid it flapping and slapping over the wet rock and finally dived on it, holding it still with both hands so I could marvel at it.

We had never seen anything like it. The *colours*! Glossy emerald shot through with specklings and patternings of glowing amber, pearl and blue. It made the brightest perch we'd ever caught seem very plain. The dorsal fin was long and flowing, the tail square, like a paddle, the body deep and solid. Its head was quite pointed and it had unusual, almost smiling lips. We had no idea what it was. Perhaps it was an unknown species never before seen by man, though this was unimportant; what mattered was that I'd caught a magical fish that weighed pounds, not ounces.

Though it looked exotic, the fish wasn't unique because we caught two more – one each – before the tide turned; and though neither was quite as colourful or as large as the first, we couldn't have been more jubilant about them.

The sea must have become less rough, or perhaps we had used up all our excitement, because we didn't need to shout anymore. Furthermore, we noticed how much darker the sea had become, and then I looked up and saw the first star. It was, inevitably, so much later than we'd thought. What if our parents had gone for a stroll round the cove to see how we were doing? They would have ended up calling the coastguard. We reeled in and hurried away over the rocks and up the cliff. I'd let the bigger fish go, but we kept the other two and hoped they might placate the emergency services.

At least the lights were on when we got back to the farmhouse, which probably meant our parents weren't fretting down at the cove. And when I peeked in through a window I saw, to my relief, that they were both still quietly reading. We breezed casually in, and before Mother had a chance to say anything, held up our fish, which had exactly the desired effect. They were baked in a pie next day, but not before they were weighed at just over two pounds each and taken to the cowman for identification. He declared them to be mullet, but I discovered later that he was wrong. They were ballan wrasse, and for the next few summers, whenever we came back to the sea, they were all we ever wanted to fish for.

FIFTH
CAST

This
Evening

The bay is almost brim-full and I have fished myself into a corner. Because of the minimal wave action, the rise in water level was deceptive and so I now find myself backed up against the cliffs. But it's quite all right; I knew, because of the new moon, it was going to be a higher than average (spring) tide and therefore ensured I had an emergency exit behind me, up over the cliff, should I require it. (However carefully you study the weather forecasts and the tide tables, there are three essential rules for rock fishing: 1. Never turn your back on the sea. 2. Travel light. 3. Don't carry lead weights in your trouser pockets.)

This last hour I've been casting hopefully, but still without quite enough faith, into all the deepening pools and flooding channels, yet though the sea remains placid and seemingly unimpressed by my flailings, its expression is definitely changing. Maybe it's just the light as the sun swings lower into the west; soon it will slant out of sight behind the cliffs, sending their great shadow down and across and eventually all the way to the horizon.

Because this anticyclonic weather, with a north-westerly airstream, has been settled for days the tideline is tidy. Had there been some recent southerly winds the foreshore would be littered with heaps of drying, maggot-infested seaweed, attracting lots of small fish who, in turn, would attract bigger fish. But, at the moment, the sea is merely lapping at clean sun-bleached stones and boulders, and there is nothing for it to sift through apart from a few bits of driftwood and the inevitable fragments of snow-white polystyrene. I never saw the stuff when I was a child, but nowadays I think there must be a factory that launches endless polystyrene sheets directly into the sea to fragment and drift across the world as a symbol of the power and influence of the petrochemical industry.

A dozen or so gulls and a cormorant have descended onto the sea a hundred yards out. They're not just sitting; they're skimming around on the surface, pecking at things. The cormorant is making long, deep searching dives and each time he reappears he's nearer the shore. The gulls follow, floating along behind him. Now a gannet is wheeling overhead, obviously attracted by the activity, but it doesn't dive and eventually glides further out to sea. Time, I think, to begin casting again . . .

Over two hours have passed and I'm now sitting on damp grass on the top of the cliff. The tide is ebbing, the undercliff is dark and a wisp of a crescent moon has just sailed elegantly over the south-western horizon. I should hurry home as I'm starving and parched, but the afterglow of the sun is bright enough for me to finish these last few pages while I'm still adrenalized.

For a while, before the sun went over the cliffs, I continued watching the gulls. Three more cormorants arrived and the whole busy flotilla began to approach

me, though I couldn't see what they were after. Even
when I looked through binoculars I couldn't see
anything skittering away from them, and when the
cormorants bobbed up they didn't appear to have
anything in their beaks. It was as if they were all pur-
suing just one very cunning little fish, but eventually
they lost interest in whatever it was and turned their
attention to something further across the bay.

I made a few more speculative casts, trying to
reach the place the birds had just vacated. There was
no response, and as the tide had peaked I thought I
could safely wade round to where more interesting
things seemed to be happening. However, as I reeled
up my line and shouldered my bag, I glimpsed a subtle
swirl fifty yards in front of me. It was as if the water
had been touched by a slowly meandering draught
of air which faded almost as soon as I noticed it.
After a few moments it re-stirred, advancing towards
me, weaving left and right, trailing a row of shallow
impressions on the surface, like a ghost's footprints.
Despite the sea's transparency, the light was too
low for me to see the creature responsible, yet even
as the slow ripple was smothered by a slow wave

I realized there were others following behind, and I presumed, because of their leisurely progress, that I was looking at a shoal of browsing mullet. But then a shower of tiddlers splintered into the air and a distinctive silhouette came half out of the water after them. It wasn't a mullet. It was the fish I'd been waiting for ever since I got here: *Dicentrachus labrax,* the bass.

What didn't happen next was fairly incredible. Instead of making an instant cast, I simply stood like a stunned sentinel, with the rod over my shoulder. Yet how could I hesitate when a fish had so obviously been saying, 'Cast to me! Cast to me!' It called again. The surface broke once more, though less violently, and as the small fish scattered I snapped out of my trance. Without looking at what I was doing, I opened the reel pick-up and cast, forgetting that, minutes earlier, when I'd intended to wade along the shore, I'd hooked my lure to the rod. Everything rattled and shook, but at least nothing tangled.

'Idiot!' I said.

Slipping the lure from the butt ring, I swung the rod behind me again, checked the line, and made a long cast beyond the subsiding ripples.

When the sea is like a fine glass bowl that trembles at the slightest disturbance, I can appreciate the art of the saltwater fly-fisher. He unfurls his line smoothly over the water and his fly lands with a whisper. But I still prefer the more direct, immediate and, frankly, more effective method that is lure fishing – especially when I'm using the floating plug. The particular gem I used today was given to me by a fellow bassologist, and although it has become battered and chipped over the years, it still turns a few fish heads. Four inches long, gold and black, hollow with a sliding ball bearing to extend casting distance, it looks like a startled sprat that has just collided with a rock. But its flattened, upturned chin keeps it planing splashily across the top when it's retrieved and, especially when the line is jagged, it does a great impression of a panicking prey fish. But what I appreciate most is the fact that it's always clearly in sight, which heightens the drama of the fishing. If I'm using a sunken fly, spinner or bait I usually have to rely on remote indication from the line or rod tip to tell me when a fish has taken, but with the floating plug – or 'slider', as my pal calls it – the whole process visibly unfolds. And audibly unfolds.

My first cast produced nothing but an outspreading ripple and a noticeable increase in heart rate. The second cast sent the plug slightly left and it hit the water with a sharp *splat*. I'd reeled it in quickly the first time, but now I retrieved more slowly and erratically, making the lure twitch and splutter. It was only twenty yards away when it vanished in an explosion of spray. The commotion was so abrupt and harsh it echoed against the cliffs, but there was no screech of reel to follow. The bass had struck but hadn't chomped, and though I continued the retrieve it didn't come back for a second bite. I wasn't too miffed, however, because after such an eager attack I was confident of another. Two casts later it happened, the fish chasing rather than pouncing, making a short but rising bow wave and then banging the rod over as it struck.

Though it can be testing and tedious to have to wait all day for a fish, when it comes, *if* it comes, it is always the most miraculous fish that ever swam the sea. Just the sensation of it along the line is enough to make a rainbow arc over the waves and the gulls to sing like a choir of angels. But of course there can be no rejoicing until it comes safely ashore.

The reel made a lovely ringing screech, though from the speed of the fish and its rapid changes of direction I could tell it wasn't a monster – not that I cared. I was just happy to have made contact. The bass – it *had* to be a bass – swept to the left where a ridge of rock came to within inches of the surface. Was it going to vault the rock? I was using eight-pound line and a carp rod, which is perfectly adequate in normal conditions, but obviously I didn't want the line slicing over an edge and so held on perhaps a little too hard. The rod kicked and lunged, but there was no despair and I suddenly had to wind rapidly as the fish turned again and came at speed along the rock line towards me. It circled close in, beautifully visible in shallow water. I bent down to pick up my net, giving the bass an inch of slack that it used to turn and thrash away again. Everything held, however, and I led the lovely thing over the mesh, where it lay quiet but still wild-looking, its big gold-rimmed eye staring defiantly, its fins bristling. When I lifted it up I felt its voltage returning and half expected lightning to spark from its silver scales.

At just under two feet long it was bigger than it had first looked in the water, and it must have been over four pounds – a satisfactory size for a bass and certainly big and bright enough to fill in the blank in my day. I haven't got it in my bag now, however. Commercial exploitation with low and often disregarded size limits means there are not enough bass in the sea to allow me to take everything home, even though they're delicious. One or two a season is my limit, but never the first fish and certainly never the biggest.

I held this evening's magic at the sea's edge until it burst out of my hands and disappeared down a tunnelling swirl.

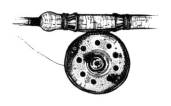

SIXTH
CAST

*Home
from the
Sea*

Having spent all yesterday staring at the sea, the inland world looks intensely static this morning. Beyond my window, the trees and hills seem to have vitrified overnight, while, at the same time, a vaguely rippling blueness still lingers behind my field of vision.

A friend of mine who used to be in the merchant navy once told me that when he returned from a voyage, after the inevitable few hours' ground sway, it sometimes took several days before he adjusted to the fixed appearance of everything. The sea may have been calm yesterday, but it was never still, always gently swirling and flexing; and though I was only watching it for about nine hours, its after-effect explains what my friend meant when he said that the land seemed asleep when he came ashore.

Half a century ago, when Nick and I came home from our first coastline casts, I don't think we noticed any difference in the general appearance of things, at least not to begin with. We were, anyway, in too much of a hurry to make a fresh start at the local pond, where a great mystery seemed closer to being solved now we'd become successful anglers. And, of course, we wanted to tell all our fishing pals about sea monsters. But when we eventually arrived on the banks, the pond looked almost comically small. Had it shrunk in a drought? The water level seemed unchanged, yet the willows that had always been too far to reach from our favoured fishing spot now looked to be within touching distance, and all the overgrown, secret corners appeared perfectly accessible. Furthermore, having fished amongst waves and tidal currents for the previous few days, it was almost irritating to watch how politely our floats stood on the flat unbroken surface.

We were not fishing for small stuff – we were using big baits and sea hooks to avoid the tiddlers and, hopefully, tempt one of the legendary carp. But though this had been an exciting prospect, after an hour – or maybe half an hour – of complete inaction, we had to keep reminding ourselves what we were trying to achieve. We knew there were carp bigger than anything we had caught in the sea but, ultimately, that fact was not sufficient; it may have been true, it may have made the pond's comparative smallness seem more fantastic, but after the drama of the sea it was not, for the time being, good enough.

The school holidays were almost over, but there was still time for more fishing. Though we lived too far from the coast to contemplate a day trip, we could, instead, cycle to our nearest river, where at least there would be movement and flow. We'd save the pond till September – or at least that was our intention – but, according to my fishing diary for that year (1959), we did not return for the rest of the season.

Although I now live much nearer the sea than when I was a boy, it is still nearly thirty miles away, and therefore I can't just slip out for a few casts whenever I feel like it. Today I have a magazine article to write, and if I stopped scribbling in this notebook and got my head focused, I might finish it by teatime. Then, if I'm lucky, I might be able to sneak away to one of my local waters this evening. Being late July, I still feel it's too early for the rivers, but I might be tempted as I don't think I'm capable of watching a float on a pond at the moment. However, the contrast would be interesting – the contrast of atmosphere rather than any difference in the actual fishing. And remembering how it was when Nick and I returned to the village pond, I'm curious to see if my reactions are similar today.

It's now nearly midnight. The house is asleep, which is unusual at this hour, especially as the school and university holidays have started and all four of my children are at home. A cup of tea steams next to my notebook, the window is open and cool air spills into my room smelling of wet grass. It's raining, but only softly, and it was not raining a few hours ago, when I was fishing the tench pond. Though there were a few clouds building then, the sunset was still radiant, if a little yellowish, and afterwards the crescent moon was bright over the woods.

Despite the fact that the sea's hypnotic after-effect had worn off by the time I was walking across the fields towards the water, it still seemed as if I was entering an alternative dimension. Firstly, there was the difference in the actual feel of things – the soft grass of the fields, the spongy moss along the banks, when everything by the sea was hard rock or grinding pebbles. The air was also softer – heavy with the green-tea scent of reeds, meadowsweet and tepid water; by comparison, the sea air was dry and sharp. Then there were the different sounds. Though the sea had been calm, there was a constant slow wash of wavelets against rock and, recalling this, I expected a contrasting silence, but I'd forgotten about the birds: despite the fact that the nesting season was almost over, the place was loud with their songs. A thrush, the most strident of songbirds, was calling from the top of a bankside oak; two blackbirds were in competitive conversation in the willows; rooks were shouting from the woods; moorhens and coots scolded each other from the reed beds. Compared to this, it was the sea that was silent. All day there'd been just an occasional call from a passing gull or oyster-catcher, but seabirds don't sing and there were no other sounds apart from the quiet murmuring of the tideflow.

The sea, though smooth, reflected an infinite variation of blues and greens, light and shade, yet, especially at high water, there were few details to actually focus on. The one-acre pond, however, was dense with detail: mosaics of lilies, delicate curtains of willow, screens of reeds, strings of bubbles, the letter 'O' endlessly repeated where a shoal of small fish was mouthing the surface. And behind everything, the perfectly mirrored, inverted landscape.

I appreciated the long light rod, the fine line and the simple centre-pin reel after the heavier tackle I'd used yesterday, and, contrary to expectations, it was a pleasure just to sit on the grass and watch a float moored next to the lilies. All my life, at different still-waters across the country, I seem to have been very happy simply staring at a painted quill, even when the only result was mild self-hypnosis rather than a fish. There were fish this evening, however.

The sinking light and approaching rain made for ideal conditions and my float slid away six times – twice for a pair of golden crucian carp, thrice for muscular green tench and once for a bland half-pound roach. I fished until the quill and then everything else was finally submerged by night's incoming tide, and I left the pond echoing to the call of an owl.

So, tonight's excursion was a balancing between two very different worlds, the one intimate and familiar, the other remote and more unknown. Back at home now, able to think more objectively, I'm sure I'll always be able to savour the former, always value it as a kind of secret door where I can slip away and find a quiet refuge. Yet though the lakes and pools that surround me here are very old and lie in an especially lovely landscape of hills and woods, there are moments when I find their charms too predictable, too constrained; then I think of the sea – uncontainable, unstable, unfathomable, whose coastline is far more ancient than any bankside and whose often tranquil appearance belies an authentic, occasionally dangerous wildness.

SEVENTH
CAST

A Rock
Too Far

It will soon be August, the month that, from childhood to adolescence, always marked my brief sea-fishing season. After my mid-teens, when the obsession with big carp began to get the better of me, I stopped going on family holidays and consequently the sea started to lose its influence. Yet, for years afterwards, each time August came around, I'd be fishing a carp pool somewhere and, just for a moment, I'd seem to taste seaspray in the air; then the tide would start running again and I'd remember something that once happened along the coast, like a traveller recalling his adventures in a foreign land.

However, it was probably just as well I – we – stopped sea-fishing when we did, because, after our initial success, not only did Nick and I become more confident, we also became completely fearless. As we grew into our teens we realized we were almost certainly immortal and could therefore ignore any of the risks that might deter other, mortal, anglers from fishing over precipices, from vertical cliff faces or deep inside a flooding cave – places that seemed incredibly fishy simply because they were so inaccessible. Eventually we discovered an uncharted island just fifty yards offshore and were lucky to survive.

In the early 1960s, when we were on holiday near Salcombe, Devon, we spent almost a week fishing along the coast before we found any productive areas. There were several interesting-looking coves with outcrops of boulders, but most of the shoreline was too smooth and sandy, and it was our experience that wrasse – in saltwater we never fished for anything else – preferred a stony, rock-bottomed environment. Clambering around a line of cliffs one morning at low tide, we dropped into a small bay with a large house-sized rock in the middle. Paddling out to it, we worked our way round its edge and piled ourselves and our gear up onto a perfect fishing platform. The rock was wedge shaped, ridged like a roof along the top, but there was a flat ledge, low on the seaward side, overlooking a swirlingly dark area of deep water. We didn't even have to imagine what might be down there.

The tide was coming in and, if we didn't want to become marooned, we knew there was just time for a few casts, but having collected some limpets earlier, we only had to thread our lines and tie our hooks and we were ready to fish. For some reason, maybe because my excitement had knitted the line behind my reel, Nick cast first. I remember looking at him as I tried to unravel myself, knowing he was going to strike before I'd got my bait in the water, though I'd actually cast, with my bait arcing through the air, when it happened. His rod top banged over and he was into a tussling fish, but before he'd landed it – using our new landing net – I'd hooked one too. Of course they were wrasse, beautiful green and black ballan wrasse, both around the three-pound mark. We'd borrowed Mother's Kodak and added the fish to the holiday snaps before we released them.

There wasn't long to wait after our second casts before one of us got another thumping bite, and then another, but maybe we'd become too blasé, or too eager, because we kept striking too early and missing the fish. Eventually I made myself wait long enough for the rod to curve almost to the surface, then I tightened and another wrasse drove down amongst the kelpy rocks. After we'd landed it, I turned round to see whether the tide had reached the foot of the cliff. It had. I mentioned the fact to Nick, but he was concentrating too intently on a developing bite to respond. We were cut off. So what? What better excuse did we need to carry on fishing?

As the sea continued to rise the fish seemed to become even more delighted with our baits. Nick got a superbly coloured specimen of nearly four pounds, and I had a couple of two-pounders and lost something larger round a rock. Then the water began to wash round the edge of the shelf and we had to shove our stuff higher up the narrow ridge. A few larger waves appeared, rolling past us and slapping into the cliff, but the top of our rock was still at least ten feet above water level and we were not at all anxious. All we were concerned about was our rapidly diminishing stock of limpets.

From far away and high above we heard a high-pitched, vaguely familiar voice, as if someone was calling from a balloon or maybe a magic carpet. It came again and we recognized it as the voice of our dear mother. We both turned and there she was, a tiny figure up on the clifftop, desperately waving, obviously trying to make us understand that only a lifeboat could save us now. Her distant silhouette made her look like a conductor directing a particularly unruly orchestra. With wild and rapid gestures, she flapped her arms around and pointed left, right, down and then upwards in an expression of despair. We were too far away to make ourselves clearly heard, but our semaphored reply was deliberately languid as we tried to reassure her that everything was under control. We climbed to the top of the rock to demonstrate how safe we were, then spread our arms and shrugged our shoulders. Mother stared, unmoving, obviously trying to weigh up the situation. From her point of view we must have looked like a pair of shipwrecked sailors, but our confident skip back to the fishing and our occasional turn and happy wave finally convinced her we'd probably not get swept away before the tide turned again.

Slowly her figure disappeared from the skyline and we could once more concentrate on the wrasse. A couple of small fish and a very greedy blenny were followed by another three-pounder. Eventually, we laid the rods down on the rock so that we could wolf down our packed lunch and drain a bottle of lemon squash. It was while glugging from the bottle, with my eyes raised towards the horizon rather than down at the rods, that I noticed the wave – a *massive* wave.

I remember the chronology of this event so vividly because its first ominous moment caused an instant misgulp and I choked and coughed out a spray of lemon juice, pointing with the bottle and trying to shout. Nick glanced up, grabbed his shoulder bag and jumped backwards. I tried to do the same, but almost stymied myself because I was stupidly still holding the bottle with one hand while scrabbling for my bag – containing Mother's camera – with the other.

I made it to the top of the rock about a second before the wave smashed into it.

We had been cautioned in the past about 'sea swells'. A boatman had once told us that 'a pocket of bad weather' or even just a brief violent squall, miles out to sea, can generate an unusually large wave – or a short series of large waves – like the ripples from a tossed stone; and on an otherwise calm summer day these waves roll in causing all kinds of mischief. There had been those few slightly larger-than-average waves earlier, but we had not guessed they might be the precursors of something more monstrous. Now this very localized tsunami swept to within a few inches of the top of our island, surged past, thumped into the cliff and came back for a second bite, though it had lost some of its mass on its return and couldn't reach so high. Two more waves came rearing in from afar, maybe fifty yards apart, but once again they were not quite big enough to dislodge us. We didn't care that we'd got a good soaking; we were simply relieved that Mother hadn't been watching – she would have had heart failure.

Miraculously the rods were still in sight when calm

was finally restored. They were both partially submerged, but their anchored lines had stopped them from being swept away. Only the tin of limpets had gone, and Nick's rod bag, which was floating out to sea. It was still in casting range, however, and after checking the outlook, I slid down, grabbed my rod, climbed back up again and hooked the bag on the third or fourth attempt. We didn't care about the lost bait as there was suddenly no desire to continue fishing. All we desired was that the tide would fall quickly enough for us to wade back across the perilous straits before another wave loomed in.

EIGHTH
CAST

*Out
of the
Blue*

The rocky island wrasse were the last that Nick and I ever caught together. We tried to locate another productive but less treacherous mark, yet despite a comprehensive coastal survey, and a few tricky descents to promising-looking rocky outcrops, we only managed a few crabs and blennies. We toyed with the idea of returning to the island and limiting ourselves to an hour at low tide, but Mother, still suffering from the memory of our impending doom (of course we never told her about our close wave), had made us promise not to. We might well have reneged and gone back after a couple more blank days had not Mother, sensing danger, surprised us by saying that we could make a day trip along the coast to revisit Lulworth. The idea of casting again at our favourite place – that shoreline just to the west of the cove – took all the urgency out of our local quest, and, anyway, could we not loll about for a bit and simply reflect on the fact that we'd just had the wrasse haul of a lifetime?

After a couple of uneventful days, we took the winding coast road to the east and, after a much longer drive than we had anticipated, finally arrived at our old haunt. Our parents set off along the footpath to Durdle Door, where we agreed to meet for a picnic at lunchtime. We walked with them for a way, then dropped down to the rocky foreshore and scrambled over the boulders until we came to the place where we'd first cast into the open sea. Had we arrived several hours later, near the top of the tide, everything would have looked the same as when we left it, three years earlier, but our timing was poor. The tide was ebbing, most of the rocks were high and dry or standing in shallow pools and, rather than revisiting a scene of triumph, it was as if we had wandered into the bucket and spade world of a much earlier childhood.

Not only had the rockscape lost its depth, everything seemed too clear and bright – the myriad tide pools dazzled in the hard sunlight, the rocks were bleached and salt seared. Yet, despite our disappointment, it was intriguing to be able to climb about across the scenery, exploring the area we had originally fished. However high the tide had been before, I realized the water could never have been as deep as we'd imagined, though there were a few deeper channels and hollows, still flooded, where wrasse could have been lurking. We tried fishing with handlines and scraps of limpets, catching plenty of small fish and nearly a lobster – which let go of the bait at the last moment – but the wrasse must have fled on the ebb.

I still don't quite understand why we didn't rockhop down to the low-water mark and fish from the ledges; however, because we'd been remembering the shoreline at high tide, and because the details of our memories were so vivid and precise, we weren't really interested in any alternatives.

We thought there might be enough time to wait

for the flood, but though we pottered about for an hour or two more it was obvious that we'd miss the picnic before the tide came in. So we packed away our only half-unpacked tackle and set off along the shore towards lunch.

The rocks eventually gave way to a shingly beach, but apart from a man and woman staring out to sea there was no one in sight. As we approached them the woman pointed and we paused and followed her line of sight. The water looked just as blue and glassy as before and there was nothing pointworthy happening in it. But the woman's intensity kept us staring into the distance – and then we saw it – maybe two hundred yards offshore but very clear in the bright light – a dolphin leaping high into the air and arcing back with an almost invisible splash. A few seconds later it leapt again – or maybe it was a different one – almost in the same place. It seemed to curve up above the line of the horizon, rising and falling with a fluid magical slow motion. It, or they, did not reappear, and the sea was once more a blank blue canvas waiting for some new inspiration.

NINTH
CAST

The
Tidal
River

The sense of physical connection with the sea that I feel whenever I'm fishing in freshwater, whether river or pool, is still strong when I get home, simply because of the well in the garden. I may live some distance from the coast, but the stream that flows deep beneath my house eventually breaks surface and runs all the way there with hardly a pause. Whenever I think of that, I can almost hear the gulls.

The rain that began two nights ago – when I came back from the tench pond – is still falling, but it will be several more nights and days before the water gradually filters down through the chalk, accumulating along fissures that eventually channel it into my well. Gravity is the constant driving force, but water is, of course, subject to other pressures, siphoning and fountaining it, even reversing its flow. I once saw a stream running uphill, though it was only an infant stream and therefore not yet strong enough to win the argument with the fiercely gusting wind that threatened to blow it back under the rocks where it was born. It was, however, just a momentary reverse, for no matter how puffed up the wind it lacked the stream's persistence, and the water was soon gurgling and tumbling again down the side of the hill, growing unstoppable as it was joined by other springs and rivulets on its way to becoming a full-sized river. But before it reached its destination it would experience another kind of reversal. Twice a day, the gravity of the moon, working against or with the gravity of the sun, would create a counter-current, flooding the river's estuary, filling its mouth with salt, pushing it sometimes miles back to a point of swirling, temporary equilibrium where there was suddenly no upstream or downstream.

The lower reaches of all seabound rivers tick and

tock with the rhythm of the tides, but between the flood and the ebb there will always be an interval when the current is switched off. The pause, or 'stand', does not last long, the time depending on the phase of the moon, barometric pressure or the previous rate of flow, but however brief the stillness there is always something mesmerizing about it, especially in calm windless conditions.

Whenever I fish a tidal river I can feel as well as see the energy going out of it as it approaches the moment of stasis. And then, after the quiet interval, its strength is gradually restored, except that everything has turned around and my line is slanted in the opposite direction to before. I first experienced this when I was twelve, fishing a small Sussex river over ten miles from the sea. There were no suggestions to my inexperienced eye that the stream might be tidal, so when my float, which had been running nicely in the current, dawdled to a stop I wondered if someone upstream had turned a tap off.

The fish seemed to be as confused as me. There had been a shoal of dace holding station, tight together between two beds of streamer weed, but as the river lost its way – and all the flowing weeds subsided into a heap – the shoal twitched out of position and began to wander aimlessly around. Within a few minutes, however, everything I was looking at changed course. My float drifted back towards me, the tresses of weed uncoiled and rolled round and the fish swung about like weathervanes, gliding into the new current. As the flow strengthened and deepened I realized the cause, yet I was still amazed that such a small river could be affected by the tide so far inland.

I did not catch any dace, and I soon lost sight of them as the water became stirred up by the change of direction. However, after a short while, when the current slowed once more and my float sat strangely poised again in a still river, I started catching a few nice-sized perch, and I saw what I thought was a salmon jumping, though I discovered later that it was more probably a sea trout. The higher, coloured water had obviously triggered a brief feeding frenzy and I must have landed half a dozen fish. And all the while the river remained mysteriously calm, accentuating the effects of any disturbance, making the ripples from a surfacing fish spread evenly from bank to bank.

Then the earth swung round a few more degrees, the moon lost its influence, the fish stopped feeding and the river began running south again, towards the sea.

TENTH
CAST

*The
Sea
Perch*

A tidal river introduced me to the bass, and though it was a long time ago, and I was only sixteen, the encounter created a little turn in my path that would inevitably lead me to where I am today. Of all the dozens of piscine species that have fascinated me over the years, only four had actually taken up residence in my dreams; but now, after half a lifetime, the bass has finally joined them.

Isaak Walton, writing in the seventeenth century, referred to the bass as the sea perch, and this old English name also appeared in my childhood bible, *The Observer's Book of Freshwater Fish*. I used to keep this book in the pocket of my school blazer so I could maintain a connection with my preferred reality, using the sacred images in the colour plates to keep me from despair during lessons. Especially maths lessons. The illustration of 'the Bass or Sea Perch' – all spectral blue and silver – shared a double-page spread with the freshwater perch – all earthy greens and russets. I was familiar with the latter because of the shoals of small ones in the village pond, but I knew nothing about the former and wondered what it was doing in a book about freshwater species until I read that it could exist as happily in an estuary as in the sea and, as a juvenile, would ascend miles upstream to feed. So, when I first cast into what I definitely knew to be a tidal river, I fished for bass.

The river was the Blythe in Suffolk, near the harbour, just half a mile from the sea, where Nick and I insisted we be abandoned for the day while our parents explored the nearby town of Southwold. Upstream of us was a broad reedy lagoon which gradually narrowed into the deep straight channel that ran down past us and beyond the timber pilings and black clapboard harbour buildings towards the North

Sea. The water in front of us was dark and turbulent, with the tide running strongly and the river rapidly reversing. It seemed we had arrived at a propitious moment for surely, as the bible said, great shoals of bass would be riding in on the tidal current.

I told Nick we were bound to catch something, but he stared into the greyish depths and said he didn't rate our chances. For a start we didn't have any proper bass bait – no prawns, sand eels or mackerel strip, only bread, which was probably not a favourite item of diet. However, the bible said that 'bass are occasionally caught using a shining bait', and we had shining baits. In our tackle bags we had a small collection of metal lures which we'd acquired over the years, not for any specific purpose, but because we liked the look of them. Now Nick tied on something in silver and blue while I chose a gold Kilko spoon with red diagonals; and as the Blythe continued to rise we began to fish.

For a while we worked our lures through the quieter water close in, thinking it too wild in midstream, but after a few minutes I made a long cast across river and, after waiting a moment for the spinner to sink, began a slow retrieve. I could feel the faint buzzing sensation along the line as the lure came back through the current – and then something pounced making the rod tip shake. For a second I couldn't believe it was a fish. Perhaps I'd simply hooked a piece of jetsamming driftwood. But then the rod swooped violently over and the reel began to sing a song that I'd never heard before. Until that moment no fish had ever taken more than a yard or two of line from me, mainly because I used strong tackle and screwed my reel down tight. But because I was fishing an open river with no visible snags, I was using much lighter gear than normal and had wisely slackened the clutch before I cast.

Hearing the continuous screeching, Nick came running over, looked up at the rod and said, 'Is it really a fish?'

'Of course it is!'

Then he ran away again, as if the situation was just too overwhelming, but we'd covered a few yards since we'd started casting and he was only hurrying back to where we'd left the net.

The fish was going with the flow, away from the

sea and towards the distant lagoon. It was pointless standing still, trying to stop it, so, with Nick following, I began to run after it, the three of us in a frantic procession that seemed to go on for miles. Despite my assertion that this had to be a bass, there were of course other possibilities. Maybe it was a shark! I presumed it was something gigantic, but then a flounder would have felt huge in the tide race.

The fish eventually slowed, turned and surfaced, thirty yards out. We saw a flash of silver before it plunged away again and made another dash into midriver. It was only a glimpse, but enough to confirm its identity and reveal its surprisingly modest size. Nick stood on the high embankment with the net, yet despite the rising river he could never have reached down to the surface. However, a few yards upstream there was an iron ladder fixed to an empty mooring point and he clambered down to water level and waited while I coaxed my fish towards him.

By now, one or two passers-by had stopped to watch the drama, and another angler, who'd been cycling along with a bundle of rods tied to his crossbar, came to offer advice.

'Got a mullet there, have you?' he asked.

'No, it's a bass.'

'It's fighting more like a mullet.'

I didn't like his derisory, local expert tone, but the fish rose again, much nearer than before, and I didn't need to say more.

'Blimey! It *is* a bass!'

It wallowed round towards Nick, who eventually reached out and managed to scoop it into the mesh without falling in. To murmurs of appreciation from the assembly, he passed the net up to me and I laid the shining fish down and carefully unhooked it. I was slightly disappointed that it lacked the luminous blue of the original illustration; it seemed almost uniformly silver, although when I looked more closely there were subtle blushings of mauve, green and blue along the back and flecks of pale gold round the head. It was just over twenty inches long and weighed around three pounds – not the giant it had pretended to be, but still, as far as I was concerned, a great fish.

Had it not been my first bass I would have taken it back to the farmhouse where we were staying, but having given me so much already the least I could do was to give it back its freedom. After climbing down the ladder with the fish still in the net, I slipped it out of the mesh and watched it swirl away again into the tide race.

ELEVENTH
CAST

Shark
Bait

If the breeze was from the south I'd be able to hear the sea rolling in under the cliffs. I am sitting on the front step of an old cottage, about three hundred yards from the cliff edge, but because of the northerly airstream the only sounds are the rippling of a nearby stream and its seeming echo in a wind-blown wood.

A couple of hours ago, just after I arrived here with my children, I followed the stream's course as it ran beneath the wood and along a tunnel of blackthorn before tumbling down the narrow cleft it had been carving through the cliffs these last few millennia. Pooling into a hollow, the stream didn't flow directly to the sea but percolated through a pebbly bank, filtering invisibly into the waves on the other side, like a person leaving the country without a passport.

Having woven myself through dense bushes, slithered down the gulley and squeezed between two almost sheer walls of crumbling clay, my first glimpse of the sea, though I knew it was coming, was like a revelation – almost breathtaking the way my outlook suddenly broadened to encompass fifteen square miles of calm unbroken blue.

To my right, the cliffs curved west into a hazy distance, while to the east they rose towards a high headland that obscured the coast beyond. Though it was mid-afternoon, the two miles of shingle beach was completely deserted. It is August. It is nearly always August when I come here because, ever since they were small, my children have regarded it as the perfect place for a summer holiday. Yet, though the rest of the country is also on holiday, this bit of coastline is fairly inaccessible and, apart from a few walkers on the coastal path, we usually have most of the shoreline to ourselves. Inland, the country is a hilly mixture of woods, small hedged-in fields, a few outlying farmhouses and, in a fold in the hills, this tiny half-hidden cottage, with the shallow stream and a grassy path running past it. Since our first visit here, twenty years ago, very little has altered in the landscape: every tree and hedgerow is still in place, the paths remain lightly trodden and the cottage retains its authentic rustic character.

Only in the last few years have I really begun to explore the fishing potential. Before then, there was always a great deal of interest in the local sea life, but this did not involve much in the way of rods and reels. If specimens were required it was more fun to use your hands. Especially during spring tides, there are always acres of accessible pools at the ebb, and, over the years, we have spent countless happy hours collecting, or trying to collect, blennies, butterfish, prawns, gobis, starfish, eels and crabs – just so we could marvel a moment at their wonderful shapes and colours before carefully returning them to their home puddles.

When my tribe was younger, it was always lovely to listen to them as they fanned out across the rocks and crawled from pool to pool, excitedly commentating on every notable object, from barnacle to anemone, tendril of seaweed to weird-shaped stone. Then a sudden high-pitched yell as the first Great Thing claimed everyone's attention. I remember the shout that went up when Alex, my eldest son, caught something that looked like an unravelled sea horse, and which turned out, on closer inspection, to be a rare pipefish. We would explore as many pools as possible until the tide turned and pushed us back towards the beach. Had I remembered to bring a rod, we might then fix it up and cast, hoping to tempt one of the bigger things that would occasionally cruise into view from deeper water. Once we saw a school of bass cutting between the half-submerged rocks, but our offerings of prawns were refused. For years, all we ever caught with the rods were pouting, rockling and small wrasse – not that these seemed anything less than splendid at the time.

Sometimes, as we waited for a bite, I would tell my fellow anglers what it was like when I was their age and the sea was full of wrasse big enough to wrench your arm off; but if things were quiet, which they usually were when we used the rods, this would only make them seem quieter. Perseverance, however, brings its reward, and on the evening of an especially big spring tide something happened to cause an even louder shout than when Alex caught the pipefish.

We had come to a deep-water bay, a few miles to the west, where a friend had assured us we would catch lots of mackerel. When we first arrived, the sea was just lapping over the edge of a high shingle bank. It looked so calm and clear that Camilla, who was then fifteen and was always more keen on swimming than fishing, couldn't resist jumping straight in. Seven-year-old Ellen tried to follow, but I said the water was too deep for her and she went off to search for coloured stones instead. While Alex and Will (twelve and nine respectively) set up the rods, big sister splashed happily around, diving down out of sight a few times and then floating on her back. I watched her for a few minutes, told her not to drift too far out, and then turned to check the fishermen's knots. As I was retying a mackerel spinner to Will's line, he looked out towards Camilla, jumped into the air like a spooked cat and yelled, 'Shark!'

I swivelled round to see a distinctive dorsal fin

homing in on my daughter. We all shouted together, but, forty yards out, Camilla must have thought we were joking because she just laughed at us. For a moment before reason took hold, the archetypal jaws from too many maneater films superimposed themselves over the scene. Then I realized that it wasn't a shark but a dolphin, an inquisitive dolphin that dived away when Camilla swirled round to look. And even if it had been, say, a mako or a porbeagle, there would have been no real danger as sharks are usually polite towards swimmers in Britain's cool territorial waters.

However real or irrational our fears had been, Camilla was not going to be persuaded ashore and she continued to swan about, ignoring our pleas not to disturb the mackerel shoals. Only when she began to feel the cold did she finally splash back to us. Asked to describe her encounter, she disappointed by saying she'd seen nothing at all and hadn't even noticed the creature's plunging departure. A few minutes later Will noticed another splash, over by a large rock. It wasn't the splash of anything shark-like, more the skittering of panicky tiddlers. While Alex and I remained on the beach, hoping for the mackerel to recover from the commotion, Will climbed up onto the rock, cast out his silver and gold spinner, and instantly hooked a rod-bender. I ran over to him and helped him land a dazzling bass – the first one he'd seen out of water. Naturally, we all fished off the rock after that, and though no one caught another bass, we discovered a shoal of big, hungry and very beautifully coloured pollack.

By the time the sun went down we had made our best ever catch from the sea, but the imagined shark remains clearest in the memory.

TWELFTH
CAST

Something
Out
There

This is a safe house, a retreat from the world. Hunkered down amongst these hills and woods, it encourages me to believe that nothing could happen here that might disturb the peace, an impression reinforced by the fact that it stands miles from the closest road and far enough from the nearest habitation to feel properly isolated. Furthermore, it has no phone, no signal for my children's mobile phones and no television; however it does have a very adequate teapot, which is brewing next to me as I write.

It is nearly midnight. I am sitting at the kitchen

table, with the window wide open so I can hear the trio of owl, cricket and rippling stream. The waning moon won't be rising till later and, from this well-lit room, the dark outside appears solidly black; but when, a few minutes ago, I was fishing on the beach, the sea looked like it was glowing.

Because of the clear moonless sky and flat calm water, every star had a trembling double. The silver curtain of the Milky Way hung down to the horizon, where it seemed to be gathered before spreading out again, only slightly less bright, across the sea. The air's clarity also made it a good night for watching the Perseids, the annual August meteor shower. Although we didn't see anything spectacular, it was mesmerizing to lie on the beach, waiting for both a fish and a shooting star.

Four of us had gone down to the shoreline at sunset: Will, Ellen, Will's pal Edwin and me. Ellen has a new book which she wanted to read on the beach, the boys and I intended to catch some mackerel for supper. With the tide flooding over the rocks, however, I thought there might be a chance of a patrolling bass, but though we fished between the boulders with both spinners and plugs we only caught a few tufts of seaweed.

The sun was beginning to roll away behind the westward curve of the bay, its reflection like a red ribbon stretching along the foreshore. The colours of the sea began to deepen, purplish blue in the south and east, amber in the west, though in that direction there were also unusual patches of paler gold. Will thought these were caused by spiralling currents of air, but I guessed they had a more fishy origin. We reeled in and walked along the beach to get a closer look. The lighter areas of water varied in size, some only as wide as this kitchen table, others the size of a tennis court. Because they reflected the twilight, they were only visible looking in that direction; elsewhere, the sea was uniformly dark. As we watched, a fish, maybe a foot long, jumped in the air through the middle of a glimmering square. The square changed into a widening circle, but it spread more slowly than the ripple which preceded it, as if the surface at that spot possessed a different kind of energy.

Had we not brought our rods, it would have been enough to simply watch this strange, gradually shifting patchwork, but having realized that shoals of tiny fish were being corralled on the surface, their fizzing panic texturing the water, we obviously felt the need to intercept the predators responsible.

Edwin has only become an angler comparatively recently and had never caught a fish from the sea. I stupidly said that his time had come, but the prospect was so incredible that he forgot how to cast and spun the lure a thousand times round his rod tip. We untangled it ('No worries – the fish won't go away.') and were soon dropping our lures nicely over the shoals and reeling back through them, where the bass and mackerel were hunting. It was a mackerel that had jumped, and it was probably chasing the tiddlers, but it's just as possible that it was being chased by a bass. Big bass like eating mackerel. We fully expected to catch both species, but somehow we failed to hook either. I couldn't believe it. Maybe our lures were too small to interest the bass, too big for the mackerel, though even a semi-salt like me knows that when mackerel are on the hunt they'll grab anything.

We tried all the patterns I'd brought, but none of us had a snatch or even a bump on the line. Possibly, then, the fish were preoccupied with particularly small fry and were not going to be tempted by something larger, especially something in metal or plastic. After dark, we gave up with the lures and tried natural bait instead. I'd got a box of shop-bought ragworm and, with the tide peaking, we re-tackled and flicked them out into the calm water.

Since rediscovering my love of sea angling, nearly all my fishing has been with the lure and very little with bait. Yet, intriguingly, I hardly ever use a spinner or plug in freshwater. What is so appealing about bait fishing, however, is that, having cast, you are at liberty to sit back, relax, enjoy a cup of tea, converse with a fellow angler or contemplate the scenery. So we lay on the shelving pebbles, holding the rods and feeling for bites, while gazing up and counting meteorites.

Ellen came and joined us. She had been sitting further along the beach, only visible because of the pale blue glow from her mobile phone. She had discovered a signal and, since it had become too dark to read her book, had been texting her friends. We counted fourteen shooting stars in about twenty minutes, though all but three were brief and faint. The fish were as unimpressed with ragworm as they had been with artificial lures and it seemed we'd be having pizza instead of mackerel for supper. Unsurprisingly, everyone was getting hungry and eager to get back to the cottage. Will and Edwin reeled in, but I said that if they could put the oven on, I would have a last cast.

'If you're not back in half an hour,' said Ellen, 'we'll eat your pizza as well as ours!' (Surely that's the sort of thing only a parent should say?)

They crunched away across the beach and I was left in near silence: just the whispered rhythm of small slow waves and, far off, an occasional splash as the fish continued their hunting. I re-baited and re-cast, then lay back again to stargaze. Left alone next to the dark sea, it was interesting how much more presence it appeared to have, and how much more aware I was of its constant ripplings and furlings. Gradually the soft sounds lulled me and the stars began to lose definition. I closed my eyes and wondered if I could sleep while holding a rod. I was very comfortable on the ergonomically compressed pebbles. Very comfortable . . . But then a fish brushed past me, and without opening my eyes I saw it shadowing away between the sunken rocks and vanishing out to sea. A second or a minute later – there was definitely a pause – I felt a thump on the rod and the stars blinked into focus.

Something out there had nudged me awake, but it didn't come back, though I waited in the starlight till all the pizzas had been eaten.

THIRTEENTH
CAST

Atlantis

With absolutely no chance of anyone phoning me or throwing stones at my window to get me up early to go fishing, I tend to sleep like a rock at this place. Despite the proximity of the sea – or maybe because of it – I can easily dream on till midday, which is normally the time that everyone else in the family gets up during the holidays. We only sleep so late, though, because, like the local badgers, we are naturally inclined to be nocturnal. Last night, for instance, after my non-fish, non-pizza supper, we went out again, very late, to watch the the moon rise from the sea. Following the path along the cliffs, we reached the high headland that gives a clear view along the eastern coastline. We settled on the grassy top to wait, and it was like having the best seats in the house because the moon, when it eventually rose, had all the drama of a great actor making a final appearance. It may have lost much of its brilliance and been only half the moon it was a week ago, but it was still able to hold a (small) audience in rapt silence, while the stars around it faded in its light. And, of course, it was still drawing half a planet of sea towards it.

When I first peered straight down over the cliff edge, I had seen, in the dim moonglow, the half-exposed rocks of mid-tide, but after the moon had risen higher the shape of an entire reef was defined by the glitter of small waves breaking around it. Maybe it was simply the effect of a sparkling outline against an almost black background, but the more I stared the more I convinced myself I was looking at the remains of some ancient man-made structure, with rows of boulders seeming to indicate the positions of now-collapsed towers, walls and bridges, the last fragments of which extended far out to sea. I said we'd discovered an English Atlantis, though everyone else said no, it was just a pile of rocks.

From the foot of the cliffs, in daylight, it was true that the reef never seemed anything more than a jumble of boulders strewn across the shoreline, but from directly above it not only looked to me like the foundations of a drowned city, it also revealed wonderful fishing potential, with the causeways and broken peninsulas making ideal casting positions.

We came back down again to the cottage, which was still in shadow, and where the glow-worms dangled on the grass blades along the path. Everyone was soon asleep, and I dreamt, rather predictably, of a cathedral standing far out to sea and being destroyed by gigantic waves. When I woke, I thought the dream had been telling me that the weather was changing, but beyond my open window everything was calm and still, and the sun was glowing on my half-drawn curtains. It felt early. It *was* early. Seven thirty is crack of dawn if you go to bed at three. But then I remembered how good the reef looked last night and realized that, if I sneaked out without telling anyone, I could be fishing there in half an hour. So, after the essential cup of tea, I left a note on the kitchen table and slipped out into the bright morning.

Picking up my rod from the garden hedge where I'd stuffed it last night, I set off along the path to the cliff edge. My first glimpse of the sea completely washed away the last traces of sleep. It was, as before, calm and blue, but this morning it also had – and still has – a different kind of expression, though this might simply have been because the air – there was no breeze – was leaning now from the west rather than the north. The smell of it was almost musky.

I made my way down to the deserted beach and began heading towards the reef. The fact that I'd never really explored it before, that I'd only decided last night to fish my way across it as far as I could, was obviously an intriguing prospect. I had fished its western edge in previous years, but never caught anything at all; today, however, I approached it with a wonderful, almost visceral optimism.

As I clambered onto the first big boulder, a bird dropped down from halfway up the cliff. It levelled out and swept overhead, revealing itself as a peregrine falcon, which, of course, was a good omen. The tide had just turned from the ebb, so most of the rocks were still dry and therefore safe to skip across as I followed a line of them, like stepping stones, out into a wide shallow lagoon. The water was very clear, and though the lagoon was open to the sea along its western side a ridge of exposed rocks to the south sheltered it almost completely from any waves.

For a while I sat on a flat slab and, through polarizing glasses, watched for any signs. The water was, then, only a yard or so deep and in the bright sunlight I could admire a submerged rock garden blossoming with different-coloured and -shaped seaweed – crimson streamers, pink bouquets, sepia stars – and, darting amongst them, numerous tiny, semi-transparent fish and larger but completely transparent prawns. A sharp, deep-sounding splash sent ripples across the surface on the seaward side, and I guessed my friends the bass were on the hunt. I stood up and scanned the water with binoculars, but there was nothing swimming in my vision until I put the binoculars down and saw five grey-backed shapes gliding over the seaweed just a few yards away. They were all about two feet long – maybe four or five pounds apiece – and, with the sun behind me, I could see them in every detail – the bold texture of their scales, the reflected light along their bellies, their round, black, all-seeing eyes. As a completely static form on a rock I was no threat to them, but I should have let them sweep almost out of sight before I bent down to pick up my rod. As soon as I moved they flinched simultaneously, turned and vanished like smoke.

Though I dratted myself for being impatient, I was certain that, even if the quintet didn't return, there would be other hunting parties and possibly one or two larger solitary specimens. In the boulder-strewn shallows, the floating plug – the 'slider' – was obviously the most effective and practical lure to use. I began making long searching casts, skidding it back across the surface, expecting a response each time and wondering why nothing happened. The water level was beginning to rise, but I had plenty of time yet before I needed to retreat. Maybe the fish were not ready to chase a big splashing lure and needed more depth around them, or maybe, like yesterday, they were preoccupied with tiny fish. But if the slider wasn't working, I could try a different kind of imitation. I retied with a small pear-shaped silver and blue spoon and, second cast, something snatched it as soon as I began the retrieve. I saw a swirl and watched the line slice away to the right. The rod bent round after it, making a series of sharp, extra downcurves in response to the fish's rapid tail-swipes. It was a bass, and a feisty one, though it didn't steal more than a few yards of line as it tried to wrap me round various sunken boulders. When it finally rolled on the surface, two rod-lengths out, its submarine grey turned a bright metallic green and silver in the sunlight – and then I brought it plunging over the net and out, a fish of exactly twenty-four inches, just like the ones I'd seen earlier.

It was a good-looking specimen and the children would have been impressed if I'd taken it back for lunch, but on a day like today we'll surely fill the fridge when we go searching later on for the more numerous mackerel. After a last admiring glance, I slipped it back and watched it dive away under the ripples.

It's a testament to my lack of enterprise that I only explored a fraction of the reef, that I was happy enough at the end of the first causeway to forget my vision of Atlantis and my grand idea of fishing as much of it as possible before the tide turned. But why spend time searching if you've already discovered a perfect casting position? Now, most of the reef is underwater and waves are sweeping across the lagoon. I'm sitting here on the last outcrop of boulders, scribbling in my notebook, thinking about the habits of bass, still watching for them but also gradually succumbing to the idea of the kettle and the kitchen table. However, before the tide pushed me back here, I had two more chances, both on the blue and silver spoon. Not more than five minutes after I released the first bass, I hooked another, probably from the same patrolling shoal as it was about the same size, though maybe a bit slimmer. And then, just after I'd splashed back a few yards to a higher-level boulder, I hooked something much bigger. It took the spoon with a tremendous cane-creaking heave and the reel yelled for maybe seven or eight seconds before I could silence it. Far out, on the seaward side, I saw a flat spot spreading amongst the ripples. The rod stayed fixedly bent, as if I'd hooked a rock, but, winding down, I eased the fish back and felt it slowly turn and come steadily round towards me. There was another walloping plunge – and that was it – the hooks slipped, and some great marauding bass sailed free.

FOURTEENTH
CAST

*The
History
of a
Plug*

have a new fishing bag. There is nothing materially wrong with my old one, except that it looks like something excavated from a First World War trench and smells like a stale sardine sandwich. Also – sorry, old bag, but I must be honest – it was never very comfortable to carry over my shoulder for long distances, especially when crammed with tackle and bait. My new bag, however, does not only have a greater capacity – I can fill it with tackle *and* tea-making equipment – it is so comfortable when slung across my back that it seems almost weightless.

We had to drive to the nearest town for some

mackerel spinners and a few essential provisions, and I happened to spot the bag – a leather and canvas Ameribag – hanging up in a shoe shop. It looked perfect for rock fishing and, though it was quite expensive, I had to have it. Now I've just emptied the contents of the old one onto the kitchen table, and picking through the detritus of tackle, rusted tins and screwed-up fishing permits is just as evocative as leafing through the pages of an old diary.

This float, for instance, a crimped red and green goose quill, takes me straight back to a pool on the Dorset Stour where, on a long-ago March afternoon, it slowly disappeared in pursuit of a rather special perch. This day ticket, issued in 1981, is still valid because just by looking at it I'm standing once more by the enchanted lake it gave me access to. And this chipped, faded gold plug, the one that looks like a startled sprat, reminds me of the moment that began my sea change.

The lure was once the property of a friend, Matt, who used to fish the Hampshire Avon with me for barbel. But then, about nine years ago, he veered towards the coast because his parents had bought a holiday house overlooking a small south-western harbour. After a while I began getting a few postcards from the seaside, telling me that he'd been exploring the coastline in a motorized dinghy. He'd started fishing for bass, a fish which he'd first caught when he was a boy, but their rediscovery, he said, gave his angling a new edge, offering him something that was not only different from anything in freshwater but also seemed more authentic.

Matt invited me down, with my tribe, to share a summer week with him and his family. We loved the house and the quiet harbour almost as much as we love this place, but though I hadn't any strong desire to go boat fishing in the briny, Matt insisted I should have at least an evening after the bass. So, while his wife, Helen, bravely took charge of six children, the skipper and I chugged out of the harbour in a two-man inflatable, heading towards one of the local hot spots, a mile along the coast. I had never fished from a dinghy before, but could appreciate its advantages immediately. It was superbly manoeuvrable and with its shallow draught could easily skim round reefs and bays and, with the outboard cut, drift gently across inlets, gulleys, into caves or between boulders. We were able to fish places not only inaccessible from the shore, but out of bounds to other types of boat.

Before we'd left harbour, Matt suggested we fix up the rods and tie on our lures. I didn't have anything suitable, but Matt handed me this comic-looking buoyant plug, saying it was of a type that, over the previous seasons, had proved the most effective out of all his other, more colourful patterns.

'Cast it well out,' he said, when we reached the first mark, 'and wind it across the surface erratically, making it imitate the action of a jittery fish.'

I tried to imagine how the lure would look from a bass's perspective and thought it would only deceive if the fish were already chasing small fry. But whatever happened, it was exciting to be able to always see how the lure was working, knowing it might be snatched at any moment.

The sea was calm and grey, with just a gentle swell and a steady tidal curent taking us slowly east along a line of cliffs. As we cast across all the likely places, we noticed a few gulls descending onto a spot a quarter of a mile offshore and hoped they might have betrayed the position of a shoal. We went to investigate, switching off the engine a short distance from the bobbing seabirds and drifting gradually towards them. They were mostly paddling about, looking down but not attempting to peck at anything. Something must have attracted them, yet there was nothing overtly fishy going on. The water was deep, and just as Matt said he might try a sunken lure there was a sudden upswirl at the end of my line. For a second I wondered if it was simply a delicious coincidence that a fish had surfaced just there, but I continued the retrieve, albeit a little slower, and within a few seconds the fish came back. It visibly dashed at the lure, turned as it grabbed it and made a lovely crunching splash as it dived.

It wasn't a big fish, but it felt like one as it went down and stayed deep for a long moment. Its rapid, angular changes of direction, however, indicated its modest size, though, as it was a bass, I didn't care about its dimensions. When I'd got it swirling calmly on the surface, Matt leaned out with the net and gently scooped it up – a glittering specimen of around three pounds.

Amid the rejoicing – it was, after all, only my second bass ever – Matt re-cast, with the floating plug still on his line, and hooked a bass of his own. Though it was about the same size as mine, he held onto it more firmly, gave it hardly any line, and soon brought it over the net. He got two more, one of them a four-pounder, and I hooked something that pulled me half over the side as it powered away, jinked and rolled free. The plug was unmarked and unmangled when I reeled it in, but Matt said it was inevitable there'd be a few losses, especially with barbless hooks, but it was aggravating that the ones that got away often *were* the biggest.

Now, five years later, after somehow surviving my many miscasts and mishaps, the same lure is as effective as ever. It is more chipped and scratched and dented than it was, and it has its off days; but though I've taken a few other fish on different kinds of lure, this one, lying here on the kitchen table, has charmed the most. Thanks to the generosity of its previous owner, it was my key to the sea.

FIFTEENTH
CAST

*Mackerel
and Old
Oak*

Last night I heard the sea from the cottage for the first time this week. There was still no noticeable breeze, and I wondered if some new weather was coming up from the south, shepherding the waves more firmly into the cliffs. The sound was so faint, however, that I could only hear it if I held my breath. Now it's morning. Nothing has changed, though I can't hear the sea anymore. The trees stand motionless beyond the garden hedge, the sky is still clear and the sun is beaming once more through the open window. It seems quiet, but there are just enough background disturbances to drown out any wave sounds. Swallows are twittering, gulls are keening, cattle are stumbling about under the trees.

I wanted to write up last night's events as soon as we got back from the beach, but because of supper – which was special – and then the drowsy feeling that it had been a long and satisfactory day, I turned my light out only a few minutes after midnight. The children were almost anxious about me! Now, as they sleep on – god knows what time they came to bed – I can pen down yesterday before it gets buried under today. With my new bag jingleful of small tin spinners, we got down to the shore about an hour before sunset and headed away from Atlantis, towards the less rocky area.

Though there was no breeze, the sea was somehow more energized than when I'd fished in the morning. It also looked less blue than before – blue shading to green. Once again, Ellen said it was more fun watching us flailing around than fishing herself, and anyway she wanted to finish her book.

There were no obvious signs of feeding fish, but as we walked along the pebbles we came to a spot where I said, for no particular reason, 'This is the place.' I cast out a little silver and orange spoon, but, being so light, it didn't fly more than twenty yards. Next cast I gave the old rod a bit of a punch and the lure went far enough because, on the retrieve, I felt a sudden bump on the line.

'That was a fish!' I said. 'Cast here!'

Edwin dropped his spinner just beyond the waves, something grabbed it after about three turns of the reel, the little rod bent like a reed stem and he finally got his first fish from the sea – a mackerel, green and gleaming like an emerald.

For the next half-hour, before the shoal moved further out, we landed over a dozen more, all good eating size. At one stage Will, Edwin and I were all playing fish simultaneously, and then I hooked a mackerel that was almost twice the size of the others and which, when it first dived away, made me think it was a bass. It reminded me that big bass eat mackerel and so, having caught more than enough for supper, I snipped off the spoon and cast again with the floating plug, hoping to lure something tremendous up from the depths. The sunset smouldered like a bonfire going out over the cliffs and the sea lost its colours, while the bass-shaped dream kept me casting till dark, without result.

It must have been nearly ten o'clock when we finally headed back up the steep path to the top of the cliffs. As there was no moon the path all but disappeared under the dense blackthorn and we were guided more by memory than sight until we reached the stile at the edge of a field, where a glow-worm showed us the way home. Over the field was another thicket of low trees and bushes with a wooden gate across the path. Earlier in the day, on my way back from Atlantis, I'd met a couple of farm labourers hauling the ancient, rotten gatepost out of the ground, and by the time we went down for our evening's fishing the post had been replaced and the gate rehung. But as we approached the spot once more, in near-total darkness, we wondered if we'd come across a glow-worm festival.

There appeared to be a hundred soft greenish gleamings on the ground, but when we looked closer we realized they were too faint and irregular to be glow-worms. Ellen switched on her phone (We never carry a torch at night – it ruins your night vision.)

and its blue glare made the the strange illuminations disappear. All we could see were a few scattered fragments from the old gatepost. When the phone was switched off, the elfin lights returned; and we could see now it was the wood chips that shone – their century-old buried decay sparked by oxygen into some kind of bioluminescence.

We each took a finger-length splinter back to the cottage. On the kitchen table, under lamplight, they were just bits of crumbly, bread-soft oak, but in the dark again they looked magical. I couldn't, however, make supper by their glow, so Will carefully bagged them up and put them away while I cleaned the fish. I poached five mackerel in saltwater with a big dash of wine vinegar and served them with rocket salad and a thick slice of granary bread, all washed down with a chilled and very dry bottle of Devon cider. It was almost the perfect fisherman's supper, which could only have been bettered if we'd cooked it on a fire of driftwood down on the beach and eaten it to the chant of the waves.

When I eventually turned in, I put a chip of the oak on the bedside table next to me and it glowed in the dark like the ghost of a candle. But in the small hours, when I woke from a dream about a strange harbour, its light had faded completely.

SIXTEENTH
CAST

*The
Void
Sea*

I crept out again while everyone was sleeping, and when I stood on the cliff edge the sea had a darker look about it. A slight breeze had sprung up from the south, carrying the smell of dried seaweed, but the waves below me were not much larger than before, with only a few trailing surf. The air was very clear, sharply defining the curve of the horizon, which, maybe because of the bright sky, made the sea look like another planet, a binary, sister planet, rising up, coming very close. And of course the sea *is* another world, and the incoming tide is when our two orbits converge. Walking the beach just now, I came across several examples of alien life scattered along the shoreline: the hollowed-out carapace of a crab, razorshells, the decapitated head of a conger eel, the bones that a fish had faded from and, washed up high on the stones, a huge jellyfish whose lovely free form had been squashed into a glassy smear by our gravity.

Maybe there was an unexpected tidal surge last night because, on my way up to this favourite rock, where I'm now sitting, I have followed an almost unbroken trail of tideline debris. Besides the expired sea creatures, there were broken planks, several odd sandals and shoes, plastic bottles, a float from a lobster pot, empty polystyrene fish boxes, tangled netting, a massive wooden cable spool and feathers – a disturbing amount of feathers, as if a shipload of geese had been torpedoed out in the channel.

I have just tied on the floating plug again, and I'll have an hour's fishing round the rocks before I go back to wake everyone up for breakfast. Whatever stirred up the sea last night may have also stirred up the bass . . .

*

If I make an average of fifty casts in an hour's fishing, and the average casting distance is fifty yards, then that means I've retrieved my lure across almost a mile and a half of water, and even though the casts were fanned out over these few acres of sea in front of me, I'm still surprised that nothing even rose up to say hello. As the water is a little more cloudy than yesterday, I thought that maybe a big silver spoon might be more effective than a surface lure, but I've just been casting that too, with the same result. Now I'm wondering where all the fish have gone, and this wondering is of a different order to the mild puzzlement that sometimes besets me when the fish apparently disappear in a river or lake. Though a subtle change in conditions can often work a mysterious spell on freshwater fish, though they are sometimes victims of poachers or pollution, it's fortunately rare for an entire piscine colony to simply vanish overnight. I may regularly convince myself that this has happened, but then, when I look again on another, brighter day, there they are once more – the carp or the perch or the barbel – laughing at me for being so faithless. But things are different in the sea.

During our stay here here last summer, I spent a morning up on the clifftop scanning the sea with binoculars, watching the small commercial fishing boats working back and forth across the bay. None was using nets, most seemed to be feathering for mackerel, but a few were trolling for bass and one boat had located a fair-sized shoal. Just a few hundred yards out, continually turning and coming round across the same small area, two men with rods and handlines took maybe two dozen fish. A few were mackerel, and maybe there were some pollack, but the majority looked to be bass, though none was very big. When the boats finally chugged back round the point towards their harbour, they had all caught a few fish, though possibly only one was going to make much of a profit. But the next day, the same boat, I'm sure, was back again in the same area, a quarter of a mile off Atlantis, setting a three- or four-hundred-yard gill net and leaving it overnight. I was too late the next morning to see what they hauled in, but a gill net is a horribly efficient method of catching fish, especially if the mesh is not too large.

Local fishermen, going out every day to make a

living, are not going to dent fish stocks as much as the high-tech trawlers that I occasionally see further offshore, but the effects are cumulative and when they use gill and seine nets they can have a devastating effect on the usually very localized bass population. A few years ago, down in Cornwall, an inshore fishing boat netted ten thousand pounds weight of bass in a single evening. The local anglers must have been sitting patiently on the rocks for weeks afterwards, wondering, like I am doing now.

SEVENTEENTH
CAST

Sublime
Choices

Back on my home turf again, after a week away, I am sitting on a fallen tree by my favourite lake, sniffing the strong scent of crushed mint, bruised nettle and wet mud. Beyond a bed of reeds, just twelve or so yards away, an enormous fish, bigger than anything I've ever caught in the sea, suns itself just below the surface. It's been there for the past half-hour, hardly moving a fin, completely comatose in this hot summer afternoon. I've been silently stalking it through the bankside undergrowth, having first spotted it as a dark shadow in the margins when I was standing on the opposite bank. It is a carp of at least thirty pounds, but I have no rod with me, and anyway there'd be no chance of catching it even if I did.

I am not here to fish; I am here to make a decision.

Tomorrow there will be a new moon, which means a big spring tide in three days' time, which means the little fish will get pushed inshore and the bass will follow. I have been invited by a friend to fish a new mark along the Sussex coast, but I have several urgent chores which need attending to, and though I could postpone my doing of them till next week I have another choice. In a fortnight the moon will be full, and Matt has invited me to fish the subsequent, even bigger, tides in his boat. If I had no chores I could fish both moons, but if a man does not eat what he catches, then he must earn his fodder by other means. Therefore I must do chores. And because I am still quite fulfilled by what happened last week – despite my fears, I caught two more bass, and Will got a three-pounder – I think I shall pass on the Sussex trip and look forward instead to another voyage with Matt.

The big carp is still there and it seems now to be leaning against the reeds as it dozes. I have a rod in my car, up at the top of the track, and if, when the sun goes down, the fish begins to root about, I could go and fetch it. There might be a chance. It is a big fish, but though I haven't caught a thirty-pounder for years, it doesn't seem to have the gravitas of those big carp I used to see. There is something almost bland about it. Yet it's not the carp that's changed, it's me. Though I shall no doubt fish this lake again some time, it seems today about as exciting as a suburban birdbath. And compared to those bass I saw ghosting past me last week, the carp seems as ordinary as a cow in a field. Maybe I'll come back and cast for it in the autumn; and at least I'm fairly certain it'll still be here as there aren't many gill-netters or trawlers on Wiltshire lakes.

I was dreaming that a man was shining a torch in my face, but when I opened my eyes I didn't even need to blink before I realized what was happening. Three days after full, almost pure white, the low moon was peering through the gap in the curtains. I raised my head and looked out at the bay. The sea was a velvety black, sliced in two equal halves by a thin track of mirrored light. Opening the curtain wider and looking towards the east, I could just make out the vague greyish glow from another, more distant source. The sun was two hours from the horizon.

Early-morning rising is not one of my favourite activities, yet though I'd had only four hours' sleep I was actually happy, after a few minutes gazing out of the window, to hear a quiet knock on my bedroom door.

'Kettle's on,' said Matt.

I dressed and, after a mug of tea and a thick slice of toast, we drove slowly down the hill to the harbour.

Everything was silent; the tide had ebbed and the gulls were still asleep on their clifftop and rooftop perches. In the moonlight we quickly readied Matt's dinghy, stowed our gear and rolled it down the slipway. With the tide out, we had to weave our way through a thicket of weed-festooned mooring ropes, dragging the ten-footer between the hulls of a dozen beached fishing boats. It would be hours before there was enough water for any of them to sail and, at least until sunrise, we'd have all the sea to ourselves.

The harbour was deserted, the air was cold and the water flat calm. After two or three slightly fraught minutes, Matt got the outboard started and we chugged out across the bay, heading directly into the pre-dawn glow. As soon as we were clear of the few anchored boats, Matt opened the throttle and we skimmed along the coast for a couple of miles, veering away from the cliffs towards a distant rock. Looking in silhouette like the spire of a drowned church, the rock marked the inshore edge of a treacherous ship-destroying reef. As we approached it, Matt shouted above the engine noise that I should think of the place as a shallow, occasionally well stocked pond, surrounded by deeper, uninhabited water. He had been fishing it all week, mostly in the evenings, once at dawn, and had caught some fine bass. On the first evening alone he took six to five pounds but, just to keep things in perspective, the early-morning trip produced only one fish, a 'schoolie' of under two pounds.

Matt cut the engine just a short distance from the cormorant-covered pinnacle, and the silence, after twenty full-powered, wind-in-the-ears minutes, was astonishing – but the wash from the boat hadn't quite spread to smoothness before we heard a plunging splash. Just a few yards to our left a bass – it *had* to be a bass – was attacking a shoal of prey fish on the surface. And then a big swirl holed the dark water on our starboard side. Rather foolishly, we'd not set up the rods before we took to the water. Now, with bass striking all round us, my fingers got twisted as much as my line as I hurriedly threaded it through the rod rings. Furthermore, I'd brought an eleven-footer and immediately regretted not choosing something shorter, with less rings, like Matt's seven-footer. He'd threaded his line and tied on his lure while I was still fumbling in the half dark, convinced I didn't need my reading glasses. Then he cast and instantly hooked a fish.

I turned to my left – Matt was sitting in the stern – and saw the curve of his rod against the moonlit sky. It shook quite violently, then held a steady bend. As the reel snarled off a few yards, another fish smashed into the small stuff right *under* the rod, and we could have doubled the drama if the end of my line hadn't slipped from my fingers and sprung mischievously all the way back through the rings. However, there was no more time for tackling up; I had to unship the net, and as Matt brought his fish thrashing to the surface, I got it into the mesh – a lovely four-pounder that shone strangely in the half light. Every scale along the flank picked out a little moon.

At any other time we might have photographed it, but even as we were admiring it another one swirled loudly on the surface, twenty yards away, and Matt insisted I cast for it with his rod. The lure was the twin to the one he'd given me years before, but my first cast was hopeless. The wondrous potential of the moment rendered me completely incompetent, though of course I blamed the shortness of the rod. I quickly reeled in again, didn't pause for breath, but cast more carefully, more smoothly, and the lure arced towards the desired spot. Winding steadily, I began the retrieve and after a few yards I saw, even in the dim light, a bow wave following the plug. We were looking into the east, where the reflected dawn clearly defined every ripple, and a dark humped silhouette, with an upraised fin, broke surface. It lunged twice at the lure, but I felt nothing along the line, though I kept reeling.

'Slow it right down!' said Matt.

We saw a dark streak of ripple as the fish struck again and this time I felt, first, a quick snatch that I thought was another near miss, then a rod-wrenching heave. The fish then made a long slanting dive that convinced me it was, at the very least, bigger than average – it turned us round in a semicircle.

Because the dinghy sat low in the water I had the same surface-level perspective as an angler wading waist deep, the same sense of the water's vibrations; I could feel the fish weaving and circling, and even hear the line as it jagged and scythed. Gradually, I raised the bass up to the surface, where it blossomed into sea foam before plunging down once more. It went under the dinghy, dived deep and then reappeared under the rod tip, its gills flaring, its fins bristling. Matt leaned forward with the net, the bass swirled into the mesh and was swung reverently aboard.

'Thank you, fish,' I said. 'And thank you, Matt!'

The bass was only brighter than the previous one because the dawn light was a candle flame stronger, but to me it looked incandescent. A superb, wild, flaw-less specimen – twenty-six inches long, seven and a quarter pounds. After a quick photograph, I slipped it back to take its chances again in the sea.

EIGHTEENTH
CAST

*The
Hour
Before
Sunrise*

Having borrowed a suspect length of carbon fibre to catch my largest bass, I was strangely reluctant to return it to its rightful owner. But the fish were still striking into the tiddlers on the surface and it would only take one more little flick and I'd surely hook another. However, Matt had been doubly generous, not only lending me his rod but also rigging up my old collector's piece while I'd been tussling with the bass. So we made a fair exchange and both cast out again at the same moment, but towards different fish. Within minutes, Matt had boated a three-pounder. Then he hooked, but lost, a bigger one. Next throw he was into another four-pounder, by which time I'd made about two dozen uneventful casts. My lure had obviously lost whatever charm it once had while Matt's had been dabbed with magic – or maybe cod liver oil.

As we drifted east on the running tide, the sea rouged its cheeks for the coming sunrise. The first gulls of the morning sailed quietly overhead and we heard the superbly dolorous tolling of a bell buoy echoing from another, more distant reef.

'A bit of sea swell must've disturbed it,' said Matt.

Or perhaps a whale had passed by.

I was only conscious of these things because nothing was happening at the end of my line, so it was completely startling when, after a slightly half-hearted cast, the rod thumped down violently on the side of the dinghy. Following the inevitable aquabatics, I eased a three-pounder over the net, and, afterwards, the plug began to fly so much more gracefully on the cast and swim more seductively on the retrieve.

'*That* was a big one!' said Matt, as a fish came up behind my lure and wallowed heavily away.

Next cast, another fish – or more probably the same

one – followed the plug all the way back to the dinghy. We could see the smooth wake of something tracking the lure as it wove and skipped across the surface, but whether I reeled quickly, erratically or dead slow, the fish remained undecided. A few casts later, a bass took confidently almost before I'd begun the retrieve, and after another rod-flattening tussle I piloted a gold-sheened five-pounder into the net.

After each slow quarter-mile drift across the reef, Matt would fire up the outboard and take us back to our starting point near the marker rock. When we first arrived in the half dark there was just a faint rippling as the weight of the incoming tide began to lean against the boulder; after the second sweep the flow was more pronounced, more audible; after the fourth the water was surging round the rock like a boiling spate river, creating a big foaming wave on the uptide edge and a large slack immediately behind it. Matt positioned his craft in this quiet pool and within minutes we shared a brace of four-pounders before being once more caught in the current and pushed on over the reef – now more clearly defined because of the quicker rate of flow across it.

As we coasted further from the rock so the silence deepened again. The bell buoy had stopped ringing, the gulls passed mutely overhead; there was still not the slightest touch of a breeze. Only the rhythmic swish of the rods disturbed the calm – and the long line-hissing flight of the lure, followed by a faint splash as it landed. The increasing light was definitely reducing surface activity, yet despite eight fish our enthusiasm was undiminished and we hadn't given up hope that the next cast might summon up a monster. We were still getting the occasional bass attack, some striking the surface quite loudly, but the fish were either missing or deliberately coming short.

Then a bass – or maybe it was a pollack – hit my lure from directly below and knocked it a yard into the air. Matt finally connected to a fish that whacked his rod down just once, but incredibly powerfully, before somehow rolling free. Seconds later I experienced the soft drag of a take that suddenly became another boat-tipping heave. I should have perhaps held on more firmly but, after seeing Matt lose a fish on a very tight line, I thought I'd try a more diplomatic approach.

This was easily the biggest bass I'd ever hooked and the reel – an old Abu Cardinal – made a lovely thin screech as the fish dived and pulled away from us. Using the force of the tidal current as much as the thrust of its tail it seemed to go too far, but I gradually applied pressure which slowed and stopped it. For a moment or two it glowered around on the seabed until, with a last jinking turn, it shook itself free, and as I watched for the plug to reappear on the surface I felt that hollowness that every lost monster creates – so that it has a space inside where it can haunt me.

NINETEENTH
CAST

*Sunrise
and Sea
Monsters*

Drifting on the steadily increasing tideflow, Matt and I made our sixth or seventh sweep of the reef. It seemed right that the current was carrying us east because I just wanted to look towards the bright upglow, where thin cloud streaks turned from chalky purple to liquid gold in the moment when, almost suddenly, the sun rose out of the sea. With perfect timing, a gannet that had been circling ahead of us dived into the reflected glare, folding its wings as it dropped, making a little sparkle of spray. Then, in the far distance, the first commercial fishing boat of the day, with outriggers, made a slow silhouette of itself. But the sun worked like a switch, turning off the fish completely. We had experienced an hour's fabulous fishing, but in the hour that followed, though we kept casting, nothing rose to our lures until, out of the blue, I took a three-pounder – the last of the morning.

Yet we carried on, because it was still early and the tide was still on the rise, but our casting had lost its urgency, become mechanical, the rods like two pendulums submitting to gravity. We didn't, however, look back towards the distant coast, or even imagine the teapot waiting for us there, so content were we floating back and forth over the reef, so happy just thinking and talking about the scintillating, elemental qualities of bass.

A little breeze sprang up, and within minutes the texture of the sea had utterly changed, the entire surface evenly stippled with fine glinting wavelets. To the west, a pale layer of thin cloud was rising across the blue, the precursor of some new weather system, and I remembered a line from the first book of sea angling I'd ever read: 'Do not trust August seas to remain calm; they can be *very* treacherous.' Had

I been alone, a mile offshore, I might have felt the need for a last cast, but though a weather change was coming it wasn't going to happen in the next hour and, anyway, I could never get anxious with a skipper like Matt, who I'm sure could pilot his boat through a hurricane.

At about the time I would normally be getting out of bed, we finally agreed we should turn back for the shore. Matt started the engine, we swung round and were confronted by a dorsal fin, a yard high, cutting through the surface towards us.

'A great white!' I shouted. There'd been a rumour that one had been spotted further along the coast, but we both knew what it really was – a harmless plankton-eating basking shark. Matt immediately cut the outboard and stood up to get a better look. It may have had no malign intent, but it still looked fairly awesome, being over twice as long as the ten-foot inflatable – easily the biggest fish I'd ever seen – and perfectly capable of capsizing us if it didn't look where it was going. But it was obviously aware of us because as it approached it suddenly dived, leaving a glassy smoothness spreading out all round us. And even though we were in comparatively shallow water it somehow disappeared completely.

But then, about three hundred yards to the west, I spotted another one, slowly weaving its way just below the surface, its snout, dorsal and tail tip clearly visible. Matt fired the engine again and this time we got right on top of a smaller – maybe twelve-foot – specimen. But just as Matt was leaning forward, focusing his camera, it swirled away and all he photographed was a blurred tail in a shower of spray.

It was only twenty minutes from the beautiful wilderness to the noise, bustle and ice creams of a Wessex coast harbour. The fishing boats were swaying jauntily on the flood, ready to sail, and we threaded our way between them until we reached the slipway, where we heaved the dinghy ashore.

Along the harbour wall there were three boys fishing. They had their backs to us and were utterly absorbed, even though other children were diving off the wall into the deep water. As Matt uncoupled the outboard, one of the boys caught a crab, which provoked only muttered interest and some laughter, but as we were packing the rods and tackle into the car there was an excited shout and we turned to see the same small angler reeling in a green, hand-sized wrasse. The others left their rods and crowded round to see it, gazing down at the little fish as if they were witnessing a miracle.

TWENTIETH
CAST

Seascape
With
Broken
Rod

What is happening now confirms my heresy. It is autumn – the last week of October, in fact, a time which usually marks the start of the best conditions on my local rivers. I have been like part of the fauna of those rivers for nearly thirty years, and always the best fishing, for every species except salmon and trout, began in the autumn. Yet here I am now, not back on the riverbank but by the sea. My former freshwater self, the one who only visited the sea in August, would probably be slightly amazed to find me here, while my freshwater friends probably think I've just wandered somewhere upstream; but I couldn't be more down-stream.

Apart from Matt, who is coming for a day's fishing tomorrow, I have a week – a whole week – with only the sea for company. And if this coastline was quiet when I was here in the summer, it's completely deserted now.

The weather is calm and clear. Last week it rained and stormed for days on end and I began to wonder whether my carefully planned escape might not end up as a week of semi-hibernation, watching water gushing from thatched eaves while reading and writing in bed. Although that would, anyway, have been perfectly acceptable, the conditions began to change yesterday and, apart from a storm rumoured to arrive around midweek, I should be able to fish every day.

I have been casting for an hour, slowly working my way up the beach towards the ruins of Atlantis, where I've settled down for a moment of bliss with a teapot. Tea made on the shore always tastes better than tea made anywhere else, but for the perfect seaside cup the water really needs to be boiled in a Kelly Kettle – the greatest steam engine ever invented.

A few splinters of driftwood were all I needed; and now, as the thin column of blue smoke fades away, a pot of fine Ceylon is brewing next to me. So I shan't mind whether I catch a fish or not . . .

And I didn't catch anything. But I made up for it today, because Matt brought his boat – folded up in the back of his car – and there is an obvious advantage in being able to explore *every* likely-looking inlet along the cliffs, rather than just those few bays and outcrops accessible from above. However, before we unfolded the dinghy, Matt wanted to inspect the cottage and survey the sea – and, naturally, savour a cup of tea. He immediately understood why I'd always been so enthusiastic about this place and was sorry he couldn't stay longer than a day.

We fished for an hour or so, down on the beach, but after the recent storms the water was still too turbid, too thick, for productive lure fishing, and we didn't have any bait which might have worked. So we inflated the dinghy and set out to sea, heading along the coast for a few miles to where we knew the geology changed from rock and clay to just rock.

Without run-off and erosion from the clay we might find clearer water.

Since the sunrise trip, two months ago, I'd only taken three small-to-middling bass, all of them caught from the shore closer to home. So it was a delight to be afloat again; and even though the year was getting late for surface fishing we were optimistic.

The sea began to look less milky – more the thick green of an old wine bottle – where it rolled in beneath a dramatic line of cliffs, with caves, islets and wave-sculpted peninsulas. It seemed a typical bass haunt so Matt cut the engine and let the dinghy drift inshore. Remembering my experience on the previous voyage, I'd brought a more suitable rod for boat fishing, an old eight-footer that had, in the past, sub-dued several large carp. And once again I tied on the venerable plug – now more chipped and chewed than ever.

The water was not as calm as yesterday, but the waves were billowing rather than breaking, and under the cliffs the rise and fall was less noticeable. As we floated along on the current, we came in range of a flooded cave where the sea gurgled and hissed as if a dragon was dying within. I cast into it three times, the third attempt hitting the top of the entrance so that the lure plopped short. Something swirled at it before I'd begun to wind, but the line didn't tighten. I twitched in a yard and the fish lunged once more, but again there was no contact. However, by allowing the plug to remain motionless on the surface, I finally tempted the fish to make a proper grab. I saw a flash of silver as the fish dived, and for some reason it looked miles away. But, after a short and surprisingly deep-down wrestle, the silver was in the net – a bright, fierce-eyed bass just over three pounds.

Matt had a fish chase his plug as it bounced across the top but refuse to snatch it. So he retied with a sub-surface lure, cast again towards an upraised finger of rock – and took a big-headed four-pounder. And with the next three casts he caught a garfish, a mackerel and a sea trout, which we decided was a kind of grand slam.

As the clouds lifted and the sun burnt through, we bobbed round a surf-collared boulder and began to drift past a classic smugglers' cove. Set deep in the vertical cliff face was a narrow curved strip of shingle where, two hundred years ago, a boatload of contraband could easily have been landed, to be hauled up in the dark with ropes from above. No doubt there would have been barrels of brandy, but probably there was tea as well, because it had a higher duty than brandy when it was first imported. And now there'd be tea again. It was a relief, after the constant sway of the waves, to feel ourselves solid on the earth again. We pulled the dinghy high up onto the shingle, where the sea couldn't steal it, and unloaded lunch and the Kelly Kettle. But, before anything else, it was essential to throw out our lines again, because we'd discovered a secret beach and needed to make a few exploratory casts.

There was a heap of sunken boulders halfway along the shingle where the water lifted, creating a swirling wash of turbulence that seemed to be saying the right words. I cast beyond the rocks, brought the lure back across them and a bass swiped at it straight away. But again it was just a gesture of intent, though the fish was more decisive when I cast again. Matt came running over with the net and, after a wild scrap, another three-pounder was hoisted ashore, though this one was much more golden than the first.

Matt was impressed with the action of the old rod and, because he'd never caught a bass on split cane before, he asked if he might have a few casts.

With the Kelly smoking nicely and the tea things laid out, I sat back in the warm sunshine and watched Matt fishing over in the far corner of the bay. A bass had already flung itself twice at the lure, but maybe the fish are more circumspect at this time of year because, once again, it avoided the hooks. As Matt couldn't persuade it to take properly, he started trying to reach a column of rock seventy yards out, and I could tell by his casting action that he was more used to carbon than cane. A carbon rod, especially a shortish one, has a quick action and responds best to a whip-handed cast. But cane has a more graduated action and responds better to a slower, progressive cast. I was thinking these things when Matt made a final effort to reach his target, punching the rod very hard and snapping it just above the ferrule so that the top half went flying out to sea. However, the line hadn't parted and, with the lure still attached, he was able to wind everything back in.

When he started walking towards me, he had the expression of a schoolboy who'd just accidentally javelined the PE master. But though he'd broken a favourite rod, one that had probably charmed more big carp than all my others combined, I couldn't help laughing. It didn't matter anyway because the tea was ready.

TWENTY-FIRST
CAST

Sea
Changes

The chug back west in late afternoon became increasingly bumpy as a breeze picked up from the south, and by the time we got back to the cottage there was a proper wind blowing. Matt left for home at sunset, and after his car had rolled away down the lane I walked back to the cliff edge to find that, in the hour since we'd come ashore, the sea had grown tremendously. Big white-crested waves were surging into the beach and, from the bottom of the steep path, the noise seemed deafening. A crescent moon, hanging in the south-west, tried to remain calm, but though the sky was still clear there was a treacherous look about it.

I let myself be blown back to the snug cottage, where I made a tasty supper with two of the seven mackerel we'd caught earlier, served with spinach and potatoes, and mint from the garden. As darkness fell, and some heavy weather swooped in, a voice on the radio reminded me that tonight was the twentieth anniversary of the Great Storm of '87.

The wind howled and the rain hissed all night, yet I slept deeply, only stirring a couple of times as an extra big gust rattled the windows. When I finally woke, at the sensible time of nine o'clock, all I could hear was weather, which was not disheartening but luxurious. It meant I could spend at least an hour over breakfast – in bed, of course. Then I wrote a little, read for another hour and watched the rain sweeping across the hills.

Today's storm is the kind of late-autumn weather that in the old days, before they were almost netted out of existence, drove great shoals of cod towards the shore. But even the most enthusiastic codders, like the few I used to know back in the 70s, wouldn't have been able to fish today. During a break in the deluge I put on my big coat, hat and boots and went down to look at the drama. It made last evening's sea look like a rippling pond – all of it was peaking and down-bursting and frothing simultaneously, thunderous and colossal, and when the waves *whumped* into the beach, scattering pebbles, there was a Richter-scale vibration. Though the tide was at half flood, the surf almost reached the cliffs, and I spent a dangerous but happy half-hour dodging and splashing. Looking along the beach was like staring along a misty road that was being continually sliced across with tongues of white flame. The surf didn't retreat after sweeping forward; it just melted like snow through the stones in a matter of seconds.

As I skipped about, there seemed to be an optimistic brightening in the general grey, but it was a false promise. The cliffs to right and left had only been visible through the flying mist for a few hundred yards, but as the sky darkened once more they seemed to close in around me. Then the rain came back, horizontally out of the south, and the wind threatened not only my hat, but also my coat. I turned my back on it and flew up the path, across the field and into the amazing stillness of the cottage.

At about five in the morning I woke suddenly to a peculiar lack of sound. The silence outside was so intense I thought I'd gone deaf in the night. I pulled back the curtains and could immediately see a skyful of stars. The storm had charged off into the north, leaving everything but the leaves (as I would discover when it got light). Something was glinting brightly through the almost invisible trees and I had to go to another window to see that it was just the morning star – Venus. But it was so radiant it didn't seem quite possible.

At nine o'clock the sun climbed over the hill to the east and, after the essential pot of tea, I went again to look at the sea from the cliff. It was in a different dimension to yesterday. The surface was smooth, with a blue so dark it was almost black. The curved horizon was sabre sharp, yet, looking through my binoculars, there was a pale mirage, like a thin line of mist, running beneath the long peninsula ten miles to the east. I went down to the beach and the benign calm made me laugh after yesterday's violence. The waves were small and quiet, the wind having swung right round to the north-west. The sky was cloudless, but after thirty hours of vigorous stirring the water was thick and milky – hardly perfect conditions for lure-fishing. However, with the mackerel I'd kept in the fridge, at least there was plenty of bait.

I didn't, though, run straight back for a rod and reel; first I had to finish some writing that I'd begun yesterday – and the time, which usually extends wonderfully when I'm on my own, took me all the way to four o'clock before I noticed it. Yet the sea was still calm and the sky clear when I eventually made my first cast. The tide was gently rising, there was a negligible current, and I could keep a strip of mackerel on the bottom with just half an ounce of lead. Having cast, I wedged the rod between two rocks and settled down to the next pleasant chore: tea making . . .

As I sipped and waited for a bite, a procession of very slow, purple clouds appeared along the horizon, but they'd hardly sailed a mile before the sun sank into its own reflection, allowing the crescent moon to grow out of the blue. A gull came flying low across the surface to be suddenly revealed as a peregrine falcon, which fluttered onto a ledge in the gorse halfway up the cliff behind me. I got the binoculars focused and it was staring back at me with eyes that had the same fierceness as those of a bass.

The afterglow fades quickly in late autumn, yet with the moon directly ahead of me it didn't get properly dark. But where were the fish? I was sure I'd catch all kinds of different species after yesterday's riot. Maybe the bait was a bit stale for bass, though there were plenty of less fussy eaters in the sea. I reeled in, re-baited and re-cast, keeping hold of the rod as now it wasn't so easy to see. I didn't really care that there were no fish, because on such a perfect evening ... Then I felt a quick solid tug. It seemed miraculous that in all those thousands of acres of dark water something had found me. It tugged again, then slowly pulled the rod over and I struck into a fish that thudded around for a moment or two before flapping in on a wave. It was only a dogfish, but I liked his sharky profile in the moonlight, and the small lizard eyes.

TWENTY-SECOND
CAST

*Hoping
for the
Best*

It is Thursday and the sea this autumn morning is even flatter and more evenly blue than yesterday, with just a few acres of white ripple where some wayward breeze is brushing it – and after maybe five minutes the breeze fades and the blue is completely restored. Low to the south, a small bright cloud hangs above its only slightly wobbling reflection, reinforcing the impression of lake rather than sea.

I am sitting on the empty beach in a mid-morning sun that is as warm as August. Apart from the muffled rattling of pebbles when the small waves flop down on them, there are no sounds. It is the kind of calm but dazzling morning when I feel I could stand on the shore and cast right over the horizon. I feel so optimistic about it that I think I might get my best bass of the year, though maybe I shouldn't have written that. Yet when I stood with my boots in the water just now and saw how clear the sea had become overnight, I felt justified in thinking wild thoughts. So now, having tied on the trusty plug, I'm going to fish my way right along the beach to Atlantis, cast across the lagoons for a while, then fish all the way back here again. Somefish is bound to rise up somewhere . . .

With a new spool of fourteen-pound braid, it seemed I *could* cast to the horizon. Having used ordinary mono all this year, I'd almost forgotten about braid's superior casting qualities. The extra range made me even more confident, but an hour or more passed and there was no sign of a fish. Yet I was singing to myself as I approached Atlantis, just happy with the sight of the lure arcing way out to sea, happy with the look of the morning. Then I saw a figure in the far distance – the first person I'd seen on the shore since Matt came fishing. It was a woman, walking steadily towards me. I was careful not to stare, though out of the corner of my eye I could see she was tall, with a shock of dark curly hair. When she reached me she stopped to say a friendly hello and asked if I'd caught anything. She was walking to a coastal town five miles to the west and would no doubt have appreciated a cup of tea had the kettle been boiling. It was unfortunate, therefore, that I had fish to catch. I said I was hoping for a bass before sunset; she wished me luck, smiled beautifully, and we continued our separate ways. This was surely a good omen; but now here I am, sitting on a rock, waiting for the kettle to boil, and fish have yet to happen.

There has, however, been a moment of drama. As I was working my way round a big rock, I stepped on a flat stone level with the water and disturbed some weird sea thing that had been sitting on it. It spluttered across the surface for a few yards, all black and spiky, until I realized it was only a poor bedraggled pigeon. I realized too what had happened to it. This is a dangerous place for pigeons, or for any other medium-sized avian, because the peregrines live here. The waterlogged bird had obviously been zapped by the predator, but had escaped and found shelter under a rock – until I came stumbling along. However, it would have had to make a move soon because of the incoming tide, so I can't feel too guilty about what happened. The pigeon managed to get itself airborne, flapping with half skeletal wings in a low curve that took it round under the cliffs. A fatal mistake. As I watched, something blurred down from above, there was an audible thud, and the peregrine threw the well salted pigeon onto the shingle. It was only forty yards away, and I watched through binoculars as the raptor – a magnificent-looking male – tucked into a late lunch. I'm obviously quite familiar to him – the strange humanoid waving a stick – and he didn't seem to mind me watching.

I am now having *my* lunch, though, by the angle of the sun, it must be mid-afternoon by now. Another three hours, then, before the moon begins to shine again. Maybe *that* will be the time.

The conditions being so good, it seemed incredible that throughout the long and lovely day I didn't tempt a fish to even look at the lure. I came in last night slightly perplexed yet not disappointed. And anyway that was yesterday – today is my last day and, as soon as I saw the sea, I thought my chances might have improved. Perhaps yesterday's conditions were a bit *too* quiet, but this morning the water had more energy about it, more sparkle, and there was a new breeze blowing from the south-east.

I got down to the shore early, just after the ebb; but if the tide was low, the sun was already quite high by the time I made my first cast. I wasn't however in the usual hurry to start fishing, and walked slowly along the beach, enjoying the glittering look of the sea yet also annoyed that I'd left my sunglasses back at the cottage. The plug was still on the line after yesterday and I fished it round the near edge of Atlantis for twenty minutes before suddenly deciding to change lures. I sat down on a big rock, snipped off the plug and tied on a medium-sized silver and amber spoon. For some unaccountable reason I tied a blood knot rather than the normal Palomar, even though I told myself I was using braided line and should be knot careful. Climbing down the boulder onto the flat, barnacle-encrusted stone where the pigeon had been hiding, I began casting into the flooding lagoon.

It didn't seem so exciting using a sunken lure – I much prefer to see a plug splashing across the surface – yet I felt more confident, and I reminded myself that most of the Atlantis summer fish had fallen for the spoon, though a slightly smaller-sized version. On the fifth or sixth cast I aimed the lure more to my right. It landed with a *splosh*, fiftyish yards away, and I let it sink a split second longer than before (*too* long and I would have been down amongst the rocks). I began the retrieve and almost instantly felt something bang the line taut. The rod tip quivered and I thought I'd hooked nothing more than a whizzy mackerel, but then there was a deeper, more sustained pull and the rod's curve remained fixed.

Oh *yes*, I thought, this is a bass! Though another thought said it might be a pollack, to which the optimist replied that no, this fish was moving too fast to be a pollack. Then I spoiled the whole debate by remembering that, as well as leaving my sunglasses at the cottage, I'd also forgotten the net. But I was on a flat rock at water level and guessed I could manage – if all went well.

I slowly regained line, and the fish came round, still

on my right, still deep. It turned suddenly making a terrific dive away and, mindful of the knot situation, I allowed it to take line quite freely. Grudgingly it came back, drawing closer now, surely almost in view. It plunged again and I felt a nasty grating round a sunken rock. For a terrible moment everything was solid. But the line was strong, and extra pressure, with the rod held high, eased the fish free. It swerved to my left, rose and exploded the reflected dazzle. I leaned right, steering the fish away from the glare until it materialized beautifully just under the surface – a solidly real but still not yet attainable bass, green and silver, showing the criss-cross of scales on its broad back as it turned again. The tail-swipe when it powered away seemed quite loud and sent up a shower of spray.

I piloted it round the edge of my rock and, after skipping across a smaller semi-submerged boulder, managed to draw it into a narrow inlet. Crouching down, I got a firm grip with finger and thumb round the lower jaw and lifted the fish gently out, carrying it over to a sheltered rock pool where I let it recover for a moment. It was a lovely creature: twenty-six inches long, quite deep-bodied yet perfectly sym-metrical, with gold, mauve and blue merging with the more utilitarian colours. The fins flared, it turned its armoured-looking head towards me, and I had to apologize for the fact that it was now time to be weighed – in a *bag*. The scales read six pounds, twelve ounces, and, though that made the bass only my second largest, I think it's definitely my best, because it was from the shore, on the last day of a very good week.

Still in its bag, I carried the fish over the rocks and slipped it back into the sea. It headed away from the reef, looking dark and purposeful, until a wave came and I lost sight of it.